DATE DUE			

The Survival Strategies
of a
Complex Organization

The Survival Strategies

of A Complex Organization

The Survival Strategies of
A Complex Organization

To Kitty

Foreword

There are moments in social time when certain books become not only welcome but literally demanded. This work falls in that class. It derives it's special appeal from three distinct, but far-reaching developments. On the one hand, there is the rapidly changing nature of diplomatic, economic and social relationships between mainland China and the United States. The ramifications of this rather dramatic turn in international affairs are impossible to fully assess at this time, but it is certain that much in the way of cross-cultural exchanges can be anticipated. To the extent that American and Chinese business men, diplomats, educators and others will want to know about one anothers' way of thinking, the incidences and experiences which Dr. Anderson documents will be most valuable. His long years of experience as a resident of mainland China and of Hong Kong and his knowledge of the Chinese language and of the Hong Kong Baptist College lend an authenticity which cannot be questioned.

The second development which makes this volume timely and important is the current interest in the application of general systems theory to the study of complex organizations. Within the past decade, literally dozens of volumes have appeared in fields such as social psychology, sociology and management, which include some attention to this theoretical approach. Despite this popularity, one searches almost in vain for case studies cast within this framework.

This study is thus something of a pioneering effort, one that should attract the attention and interest of social organizational specialists.

The third reason this work should find a receptive audience is its focus on induced or instigated change. Dr. Anderson lucidly describes the problems encountered in attempting to superimpose Western ways and values on a Chinese cultural base. The strategies which had to be worked out and the concessions which were in order will make fascinating reading, not only for those who are charged with the administration of denominationally affiliated educational institutions, but for those professionally interested in what has been termed the sociology of development.

It was an honor for me to receive the invitation to do this foreword. Because of my long association with Dr. Anderson and my intimate acquaintance with his work, I cannot escape a measure of excitement over the publication of this volume.

Alvin L. Bertrand
Louisiana State University

Acknowledgments

The writer is indebted to Dr. Alvin L. Bertrand for constructive advise and criticism in guiding the preparation of this dissertation. Dr. Walfrid J. Jokinen, Dr. George L. Wilber, and Dr. Joseph H. Jones, Jr., also offered valuable advise and methodological suggestions for which the writer is grateful. Intellectual stimulation in classroom teaching was given the writer by Dr. Vernon J. Parenton, Dr. George Hillery, Jr., and Dr. Rudolph Heberle and is acknowledged with special appreciation. Drs. Fred C. Frey, Homer L. Hitt, Marion B. Smith, Paul Price, Henry L. Shanklin and Paul C. Young, who were among the writer's first teachers of Sociology and Psychology, are remembered for the contribution which their teaching and friendly encouragement made.

Special mention is due Mr. Stephen Eng, and many other students and friends in Hong Kong, for assistance in collecting records and other data used in this study. The large number of faculty and staff members, as well as college Governors and administrators at the Hong Kong Baptist College, with whom the writer worked for many years, are remembered with appreciation. They were part of the interaction which provided the data for this study.

The writer is grateful to many typists, but the greatest thanks goes to Mrs. Pia Blanco who did the final manuscript.

Finally, the writer is indebted to his wife for patience and understanding during recent months. He wishes to thank the officials of the Southern Baptist Foreign Mission Board who extended his leave from Hong Kong for an additional two months so that the dissertation could be completed.

Contents

LIST OF TABLES

LIST OF ILLUSTRATIONS

The Survival Strategies

of a

Complex Organization

CHAPTER I

THE STUDY PROBLEM AND
ITS SIGNIFICANCE

The present study was planned with the hope of making a contribution to the theory of social organization. It is a sociological analysis of the survival strategies of a complex organization in a foreign cultural setting. The intention was to focus attention on the more-or-less unusual mechanisms employed by Chinese and western actors to found and operate a western-type denominational college in an eastern cultural setting. The "game" of these "players" became the serious business of forming coalitions, both inside and outside the college organization, and of engaging in the processes of cooperation, competition, accommodation, conflict, and confrontation. Both the problem under study and its significance are implicit in the above statement.

The fact that the complex organization investigated is a western-type educational-religious system located in an eastern cultural setting is the first matter of significance for social organization theory. Schools featuring western educational methods and curricula, and concurrently serving religious purposes, have played a more-or-less important part in the educational organization of the East for many decades. Clearly, special strategies were and must be followed to make these transplants palatable to supporters and clients in the East. In this regard it has been customary for western educators, as personnel from missionary organizations to be represented on advisory boards of these organizations. Also, westerners have usually worked alongside easterners as administrators and teachers in the schools. These relationships have served to add a special dimension to the structural composition of such organizations and, consequently, to the inter-actional processes occuring within them. Stresses and strains have been in evi-dence, although easterners and westerners may have had similar religious affilia-tions. Stress is inherent in these organizations because the cognitive perceptions of persons with different cultural orientations frequently become a source of misunderstandings. Furthermore, the situation is complicated because the sour-ces of finance, so necessary for developing organizations in the East, are usually the countries from which the western co-workers have come. Such an organi-zational situation calls for strategies and actions which are unusual to western-based colleges and universities. Insofar as the writer could determine no study has been done of the strategies of actors in such complex organizations.

Practical considerations provide the second reason for undertaking this in-vestigation. A report on the findings of a recent survey of more than a hundred educational-religious organizations in Asia points to the need for studies of a social science nature. The team of educational specialists from the United States and Asia who recently prepared the report were supported by the New York-based United Board for Higher Education in Asia. Their appraisal of the educational organization of this study, the Hong Kong Baptist College, (in a special section on the situation in Hong Kong) indicates that the colleges' characteristics and problems are similar to those of other Christian colleges in this part of the world. The survey members suggested that each organization should be investigated in depth because of educational and religious problems each poses. [1] It is implicit in the latter statement that other organizations, in Asia and elsewhere, might benefit from the analysis which follows. The study sheds light on a number of problems experienced by administrators and support-ers of western-type educational-religious systems in particular. In addition, other types of complex organizations with western roots in the East, of which there are many, should be benefited.

Another goal of the writer in embarking on this study was to supply the administration of the Hong Kong Baptist College with an appraisal of the inter-action milieu which has characterized the college from the time of its founding to the present. This information will make possible a more realistic assessment of the strengths and weaknesses of this social system's organizational structure, and provide a better understanding of its patterns of relationships. It also should provide guidance for the present and future planning of survival strategies.

The recent retirement or transfer of a number of long-time administrators, and teachers, and the prospect of other changes in the very near future, makes it likely that control will eventually be in the hands of men who are new to this organization and its problems. An account of past successes and failures will help them execute the strategies necessary to achieve the objectives of the founders and supporters of the college. This study, then, hopefully will provide clues for the development of new mechanisms for insulating against behavior destructive to the development of the college. Sources of energy in the form of money and teaching personnel must be obtained in the West, while contact with power influentials in Hong Kong must be maintained to assure a healthy state for the organization. In an area of the East where rapid change is the order of the day, misjudgments can be tragic for survival.

The paucity of studies of educational organizations as social systems is a final reason for undertaking this investigation. Most of the research which has been done by social scientists in the educational field has been in the areas of primary and secondary schools. However, even in these areas the number of studies available are few. [2]   It is understood that several social scientists are at present making studies of western colleges and universities, which will help to fill the gap in case-studies of this type. This study of a western-type educational organization in the East can be a source of empirical information for comparative purposes.

----

1. *An Appraisal of the Protestant Christian Effort in Higher Education in Asia: Hong Kong,* an unpublished report (75 Riverside Drive, New York: The United Board for Higher Education in Asia, 1968).
2. Charles E. Bidwell, "The School as a Formal Organization," *Handbook of Organizations,* James C. March, ed. (Chicago: Rand McNally and Company, 1965), pp. 972-1022; Betsy Ann Olive, "The Administration of Higher Education," *Administrative Science Quarterly,* Vol. II (1966-67), pp. 671-77. Available primary and secondary school case studies are: Joseph S. Fichter, S.J., *The Parochial School: A Sociological Study* (Notre Dame, Indiana: Notre Dame University Press, 1958); and C. Wayne Gordon, *The Social System of the High School* (Glencoe, Illinois: The Free Press, 1957).

CHAPTER II

APPROACHES TO THE STUDY OF
COMPLEX ORGANIZATIONS

As pointed out in the previous chapter few case studies of colleges as organizations are available. However, there have been many studies of "organizations" during the history of sociology. The writer has selected the works of authors whose approaches, he feels, illustrate the range of thinking in the field. The order of discussion is designed to lead to the conceptual approach followed in the analyses made for this study.

I. MAX WEBER

Max Weber was one of the first sociologists to provide a conceptual model for the investigation of what have come to be known as complex organizations. [1] He was interested in the distribution of power in, what he termed, bureaucracies. Weber not only saw an interdependence among the structural attributes of complex organizations but also a clear-cut division of activities in organizational positions. His discussions opened a new era in sociological research, in which such concepts as power and legitimization became popular. Weber used "power" to refer to the ability of the holder of a position to secure acceptance of orders; and "legitimization" to refer to the acceptance of the exercise of this power, so long as the latter was in line with the values held by the subjects of the power. "Authority" was a combination of the two, i.e., power viewed as legitimate. His famous classification of authority was based on the sources and kinds of legitimization employed. In traditional authority subjects acquiesce to superiors on the ground that this is the way things are always done. In rational-legal (bureaucratic) authority subjects accept orders on the basis of abstract rules which they consider legitimate. In charismatic authority subjects acquiesce to the influence of the personality of the superior with whom they identify. [2]

A number of researchers, especially those interested in the analysis of economic and political organizations, found a point of departure in Max Weber and his discussions of bureaucracy, as well as his use of ideal typologies. Weber's concepts and methods proved quite useful to them. Several scholars have made use of the traditional-rational typology to analyze present-day organizations. However, most of the latter investigators have concluded, that Weber's bureaucratic model did not fit modern complex organizations precisely.

Robert Merton provided one of the most insightful criticisms of Weber's analysis by calling attention to the dysfunctions of bureaucracies. He points out that Weber, and those who utilized his typology, tended to emphasize precision, reliability, and efficiency. In this emphasis they neglected the study of stresses and strains in bureaucratic structures. By using Veblen's concept of "trained incapacity", or a state of affairs in which a person's abilities function as inadequacies, Merton showed the weaknesses in the Weberian approach. He pointed out that an official should be methodical, prudent, and disciplined, which required appropriate attitudes and sentiments. Merton correctly stated that often these sentiments become more intense than is necessary and that adherence to rules become an end rather than a means to an end. He noted, furthermore, that through sentiment-formation some bureaucratic norms became rigid and treated as sacred. When this happened these norms failed to expedite the administration of the bureaucracy. Also, he pointed to the dysfunction which emphasis on impersonality might cause, such as the tendency for functionaries and clerks to be harsh and abrupt to clients and domineering in relations with the public which the bureaucracy served. [3]

Despite the above criticism, Weber definitely made a contribution to social organization theory. His interpretations will be evident in many of the discussions which follow.

II. PETER BLAU AND W. RICHARD SCOTT

Within recent years several scholars have undertaken studies of complex organizations. They justified their studies in terms of the criticism of Weber's work outlined above and because comparative studies of organizations had called attention to basic differences in types of organizations. Blau and Scott are among these scholars. They set forth generalizations with which they seek to explain the structure and dynamics of "formal" organizations. [4]

Blau and Scott prefer to call large-scale social systems "formal organizations" and take exception to the term "complex" which Etzioni and others use and which is accepted by the writer. The argument of Blau and Scott is that organizations vary in size and complexity, and that "complexity" is a characteristic not only of deliberately-formed, goal-oriented organizations but also of organizations which have emerged in an evolutionary process. Consequently, to them the term, "complex", is not distinctive of deliberatively-formed organizations. They do not use the term, "Bureaucracy", commonly utilized by Max Weber, Robert Merton, and others, since in ordinary language it is often equated with "rule-encumbered inefficiency". However, they have no quarrel with the term when neutrally used to refer to the administrative aspects of organization. The writer utilizes the term, "complex", for the reason that formal and large-scale seem to him to be best characterized by this term.

Blau and Scott delineate four types of organizations in terms of the categories of persons which the organization served. The criterion on which their types are based is the prime category of beneficiaries as follows: (1) members, or the rank-and-file participants; (2) owners or managers; (3) clients, or persons such as patients, customers, prisoners, soldiers, and students, who are technically "outside" the organization, yet have regular, direct contact; and (4) the public at large, or the members of the society in which the organization operates. The four types of organizations identified by Blau and Scott are: (1) mutual benefit associations, (2) business concerns, (3) service organizations, and (4) commonweal organizations. They recognize the crucial problems of each type of organization respectively: (1) to maintain internal democratic processes; (2) to maximize operating efficiency in a situation of competition; (3) to handle the conflict between professional service to clients and administrative procedures; and (4) to develop democratic mechanisms for external control by the public.

Blau and Scott utilized their typology to make comparative studies. Their approach in these studies was threefold: (1) secondary analysis, i.e., comparing case studies of various organizations; (2) the internal comparisons of different sub-groups in one organization; and (3) the comparison of separate organizations studied empirically. The authors do not arrive at general conclusions but do provide insight into the structure and functioning of this type of social structure. [5]

III. AMITAI ETZIONI

Etzioni utilizes case studies of organizations in an attempt to develop middle range theories relating to sub-categories of organizations. He conceives of the comparative analysis which he makes as a step in the direction of establishing the true universals of organizational theory. In this way he hopes to fill gaps which he feels the general Weberian model has neglected. The base for Etzioni's organizational classification is compliance both in terms of "the power exercised by superiors to control subordinates and the orientation of the subordinates to this power." [6]

Etzioni argues that modern sociology has drawn on the approach of Pareto which focuses on the hierarchical distribution of force; the Marxian approach, which emphasizes property relations; and the normative approach, which emerges from a synthesis of Weber's study of the role of ideas in social action and Durkheim's study of shared sentiments. He feels that control forces, namely, (1) coercion, (2) economic assets, and (3) normative values, respectively, are universals and serve as types of compliance, each having equal status with the other in this respect. He assumes that social relationships in organizations differ in relation to the predominance of one or the other of these three kinds of control, and uses an analysis of each as the basis for his comparison of organizations. In his studies Etzioni explores the relationship between compliance in these three forms of control and such variables as cohesion, leadership, and consensus. He deals with such factors as kinds of compliance and types of organizational goals and focuses on compliance characteristics of both higher and lower level participants.

Etzioni also discusses the dynamic aspects of social organization as the development of compliance structures over time and points out ways for further developments in the study of compliance. However, he limited himself largely to a concern for the relationships between compliance and the other variables introduced. [7]   Etzioni's studies were mainly of compliance structures in modern democratic societies, principally in the United States. Nonetheless, there is no question but that his classification and discussion of coercive, utilitarian, and normative organizations provides useful middle range statements for the study of such social units.

IV. DON MARTINDALE

Martindale, a social behaviorist, called attention to the lag in the development of a theory of large-scale organization. He undertook to revise and update social behavioristic theory of organization as a major alternative to functionalist theories, such as espoused by Blau and Scott, Etzioni, and Parsons. [8] His premise was that behaviorism takes social action, not social system, as its primary reality. He viewed man as working out social arrangements of various kinds and forms in terms of the individual and collective problems he had to solve. His approach did not conceive of an equilibrium between man and society; rather it was concerned with exploring the varied ways man goes about utilizing the resources available to him.

Martindale set forth six major hypotheses for estimating the significance of large-scale organizations for the personality and community of modern man, as well as for social structure. They are:

1. In contrast to traditional groups, large-scale organizations rest upon an extensive division of labor, the formalization of relations, and structural rationalization;
2. The basic impulses to create large-scale organizations occur in the area of group life (rather than in the total social system);
3. Large-scale organizations create the "milieu" within which they flourish;
4. Large-scale organizations transform the traditional situation of the groups;
5. Large-scale organizations change the personalities of contemporary men and have predicted a crisis in their self-conceptions; and
6. The community appropriate to the large-scale organization is the contemporary nation or so-called "Mass Society". [9]

Martindale approaches the problem of social organization from an elementaristic rather than a holistic point of view. He sought to develop the first hypothesis, stated above, by showing that division of labor, formalizations of relations, and rationalization, which he called the "critical characteristics of the large-scale organization", had their sources in (1) industrial and (2) administrative organizations. In the first instance he sought to show their manifestation as a result of organization for machine production, the scientific management movement, and automation. In the second, he sought to show the manifestation of the same characteristics in the ever-expanding phenomenon of bureaucratization. [10] Martindale feels that the above characterize all large-scale organizations wherever they appear.

Martindale undertakes to develop his next three hypotheses by illustrating three major structures: (1) large-scale organizations for the mastery of nature, such as economic organizations, (2) large-scale organizations for social control, such as governments, and (3) large-scale organizations for socialization, such as universities. This approach lends itself, in his view, to explanations of the origin of large-scale organizations, their development, and their being the consequences of strategic behaviors designed to cope with problems when and where they occur. [11]

Martindale also undertakes to develop his last two hypotheses, which deal with the problem of personality, in a world of large-scale organizations. His premise is that the "milieu" in which modern men work out their destinies is created by the accommodation and competition of these large-scale social units. His thesis is that the alienation of modern man is a product of the type of organizational world into which he has been thrust. He hypothesizes that the crisis in contemporary man's self-conception is a result of the large-scale organizational life to which he has been subjected. [12]

V. TALCOTT PARSONS AND HIS ASSOCIATES

Parsons brought to the fore the concept, "social system", as a devise to analyze social activity. [13] He defined a social system as "a plurality of individual actors interacting with each other in a situation which has at least a physical or environmental aspect, actors who are motivated in terms of a tendency to the optimization of gratification and whose relations in their situations, including each other, is defined and mediated in terms of a system of cultural structures and shared symbols". [14] A social system was perceived by him at any level from a face-to-face relationship between two actors, to intelligent behavior related to diverse types of associations or organizations, to a society of many people living together and behaving according to a system of patterned relationships. [15] He conceived that activity has the function of maintaining a social system. He and his followers largely concerned themselves with this type of structural-functional analysis of large-scale systems.

Parsons worked out five patterned ways of role-definition, or pattern variables, by which he believed he could solve behavioral dilemmas, and with which he believed society could be exhaustively analyzed, as follows:

1. The gratification-discipline dilemma: Affectivity versus affective neutrality;
2. The private versus collective interest dilemma: self orientation versus collectivity-orientation;
3. The choice between types of value-orientation standard: universalism versus particularism;
4. The choice between "modalities" of the social object: achievement versus ascription; and
5. The definition of scope of interest in the object: specificity versus diffuseness. [16]

Parsons and Bales later went into the problems of goal-attainment, adaptation, integration, pattern maintenance, and tension management in social systems. [17] The latter had a special interest in the study of small groups, and his detailed analyses of these structures pointed the way for the analyses of larger structures, such as complex organizations.

Merton, was another scholar who was greatly influenced by Parsons. Defining function as system-maintaining [18] Merton formulated the concept, "dysfunction", to identify action or behavior which was not functional. He also called attention to "manifest" and "latent" functions, respectively defined as the objective consequences of social activity, and the unintended or unrecognized potential consequences. [19]

The Structural-Functionalist school, led by Parsons, as pointed out, held that recurrent social activity maintains social systems. They however, have been subject to increasingly pertinent criticism. [20] The two major points are: an outdated, mechanistic, static, closed-system model is used rather than an up-to-date, adjustive, dynamic, open-system model, and a state of equilibrium is suggested which does not give a correct image of the dynamic state of a healthy social system. Because of the above, their models do not deal adequately with time dimensions or social change. [21]

It should be said in favor of Parsons and Merton that the functional approach reintroduced the concept of "system" at a time when sociologists were in need of an analytical tool for comprehending increasingly sophisticated conceptualizations. It seems probable that the difficulties and shortcomings of the structural-functional approach will be overcome by incorporating insights from other traditions, like social behaviorism. In so doing, sociologists may perfect a social systems model as a tool for guiding empirical analyses.

In the chapter which follows, the writer outlines his conceptual frame of reference for the study of a complex organization. It will be seen that he draws on many of the notions set forth by the scholars discussed in this chapter.

---

1. Max Weber, *Economy and Society*, Gunther Roth and Claus Wittich, editors (New York: Bedminister Press, 1968), Vol. I, pp. 48-62, 212-84.

2. *Ibid.*, pp. 212-45.

3. Robert Merton, *Social Theory and Social Structure*, Enlarged Edition, (New York: The Free Press, 1968), pp. 251-59.

4. Peter Blau and W. Richard Scott, *Formal Organizations* (San Francisco: Chandler Publishing Company, 1962).

5. *Ibid.*, pp. 42-58, 222-23.

6. Amatai Etzioni, *A Comparative Analysis of Complex Organizations* (Glencoe, Illinois: The Free Press, 1961), p. xv.

7. *Ibid.*, pp. xi-xvii, 3-67, 297-313

8. Don Martindale, *Institution, Organizations, and Mass Society* (Boston: Houghton Mifflin Company, 1966).

9. *Ibid.*, p. xv.

10. *Ibid.*, pp. 129-61.

11. *Ibid.*, p. 512.

12. *Ibid.*, pp. 513-62.

13. Talcott Parsons, *Social System* Glencoe, Illinois: The Free Press, 1950).

14. *Ibid.*, pp. 5-6.

15. John E. McKinney, *Constructive Typology and Social Theory* (New York: Appleton-Century-Crofts, 1966), p. 120; F. Nadel, in *The Theory of Social Structure* (Glencoe, Illinois: The Free Press, 1956), p.1, points out that models are heuristic analytical tools, i.e., conceptual devises to facilitate the scientific process. They are legitimate instruments to get an abstract simplified representation of social phenomena so as to better understand that phenomena. In the sense that such models have a body of inter-connected propositions which map out problem areas, classify phenomena, and analyze them into relevant units, they may also be understood as theories.

16. Talcott Parsons, *op. cit.*, p. 67.

17. Robert F. Bales, Talcott Parsons, and Edward A. Shils, *Working Papers in the Theory of Action* (Glencoe, Illinois: The Free Press, 1953), and Robert F. Bales and Talcott Parsons, *Family, Socialization, and Interaction Process* (Glencoe, Illinois: The Free Press, 1955).

18. Robert Merton, *Social Theory and Social Structure* (Glencoe, Illinois: The Free Press, 1957), p. 51.

19. *Ibid.*, pp. 19-84, 197-200.

20. See Kingsley Davis, "The Myth of Functional Analysis as a Special Method in Sociology and Anthropology," in *American Sociological Review*, Vol. 24 (December, 1959), pp. 757-72. Davis argues that so-called "functional analysis" is the same as other sociological analysis. George C. Homans, "Bringing Men Back In," *American Sociological Review*, Vol. 29 (December, 1964), pp. 809-18, supports Davis' view, and goes further to argue that "functionalism" was not a theory. Rather, according to Homans, the functionalists only set up a new conceptual scheme, a new language for describing social structure. The functionalists, he argues, use psychological explanations to answer the question "why" and, therefore, they have sociological theory that is grounded in psychological theory. He further points out that when sociologists explain social phenomena, they actually state propositions about the behavior of men, and there is no social theory that is not grounded in psychological theory. The functionalists, he says, should admit this fact.

21. Walter Buckley, "Structural-Functional Analysis in Modern Sociology," *Modern Sociological Theory in Continuity and Change*, Howard Becker and Alvin Boskoff, eds. (New York: Holt, Rinehart, and Winston, 1957), pp. 236-59; Walter Buckley, *Sociology and Modern System Theory* (Englewood Cliffs, New Jersey: Prentice-Hall, Inc., 1967); Don Martindale, "Limits of an Alternatives to Functionalism in Sociology," *Functionalism in The Social Sciences* (Philadelphia: The American Academy of Political and Social Sciences, February, 1965), pp. 156-60.

CHAPTER III

CONCEPTUAL FRAME OF REFERENCE

The preceding discussion has shown that there has been an interest in the analysis of organizations in recent decades which has emphasized the need of adequate conceptual tools. The writer outlines his approach in the discussion which follows.

I. THE APPROACH: MODERN "OPEN" SYSTEMS THEORY

The modern "open" systems approach, which provides the theoretical frame for this study, is offered as a conceptual tool for the analysis of organizations. Buckley recognizes this theoretical approach as one which closely links the elements of social organization by way of information and communication. He interposes the conditions of dependency on chance conditions or uncertainty, on coercion or constraints, and on the presence of degrees of freedom in the nature of organizational structure, and argues against the closed system idea in which relationships between the parts of a structure are likely to be rigid and fixed. [1]

Buckley sees the following attractive features for sociology in the modern "general" systems approach:

1. A common vocabulary unifying the behavioral sciences;
2. A technique for treating large complex organizations;
3. A synthetic approach in which the intricate inter-relationships between parts are treated in the context of the whole;
4. A way of looking at the sociocultural system in terms of information and communication nets;
5. The study of relations or connections rather than an entity as something real in itself, with emphasis on possibilities of process and transition as the

bases of flexible structure with many degrees of freedom, and
6. A study of purposefulness, goal-seeking system behavior, symbolic cognitive processes, consciousness and self-awareness, and sociocultural emergence and dynamics in general which is operationally definable, objective, and non-anthropomorh

Common Characteristics of Open Systems

Katz and Kahn have identified the common characteristics in open systems. These characteristics are briefly described below.

1. *Importation of energy.* In social organizations this is seen as the interaction between individuals linking sub-systems, and the renewal of supplies of energy from other institutions, people, or the material environment. In a college the interaction linking trustees, administrators, and teachers is one form of energy input. The recruiting of students, money, and moral support is another.

2. *The through-put.* The social organization transports, converts, creates, processes, and trains in the interest of a goal. This is the performance of work, which can be seen as the reorganization of some type of input. A college, in its processes of orientation, teaching, and training is performing work which might be thought of as reorganizing the input for later production.

3. *The output.* This is the exportation of the products of the social organization into the outside environment. The graduation of students and their dispersion in the community is a large part of a college output.

4. *Cycles of events.* This is the import-export process seen as a complete cycle of activity. The interaction characteristic of a system of social organization is seen as comprising a repetitive chain. The repeated events may be identified as being the same, but their character may change, or the cycle may become shorter or longer so as to alter it somewhat. A cycle of activities and events, lasting for four or five years, during which time students complete their courses, repeats itself for different groups of students, while teachers and staff members may continue in the system for much longer periods of time.

5. *Negative Entropy.* Open systems, unlike closed systems, may have mechanisms which slow down the process by which they move toward less efficiency and finally death. Actions to improve programs and to develop the system's resources are forms of negative entropy. All activity designed to improve a college would be related to negative entropy.

6. *Negative feedback and coding.* The parts of the system in contact with the external environment serve to feedback information on the efficiency and the effects of the system's operation. Those in the school who are in contact with

organizations employing or otherwise using graduates, and organizations concerned with the executing of program and curricula building receive communications as to the extent to which the school is "on course".

7. *Steady state.* This condition exists in the social system when input-output exchanges are constant and produce a sort of balance. Since input-output is constantly changing, this is not to be conceived of as equilibrium, but rather as dynamic homeostasis. That condition in which the college properly balances income and expenditure of funds, provides a satisfactory teacher-student ratio, and a proper balance between academic and other goals has to do with its steady state.

8. *Differentiation.* Movement in social systems in the direction of a greater division of labor are not uncommon. Also, there is a tendency to assign functions in terms of specialized duties. Technology is seen as one of the factors which help this come about in modern society.

In a college the increasing activities which are provided, and the elaboration of hierarchical relations as the organization grows, can be seen as a part of differentiation. The adding of departments, both for teaching and for other functions, is related to this characteristic.

9. *Equifinality.* Open systems have the ability to achieve the same on or near the same final state or product utilizing different processing or organizational steps. A college may change its departmental structure or emphasize first one requirement then another, or it may alter programs to meet special circumstances, yet give the same degree to students under both the old and new systems. The achievement of a desired final state of a matriculated student regardless of paths taken by the individual is its characteristic of equifinality. [3]

Basic Features of Open Systems

The characteristics of an open system, were outlined above. Its basic features may now be summarized.

1. *The primary emphasis is on the system as a whole.* The whole system has distinctive characteristics and properties and a unity of its own. Although the parts may be studied separately, they can only be understood in relation to the larger whole. We have in the system an emergent whole which cannot be reduced to its component parts without destroying the whole system.

2. *The system has open boundaries.* The boundaries of an open system are always at least partially open for the exchange of individuals, materials, energy, or information.

3. *The internal ordering of component parts of the system and of the rela-*

tionships between them is such that the patterns and degrees of the ordering may vary. The patterns and degrees of interdependence and interrelatedness among the sub-units of an open system can never be seen as static.

4. *The process of homeostasis is assumed to be operating.* Homeostasis, the process of self-maintenance, serves to counter disruptive forces in an open system. The key features of such systems, such as boundaries, patterns of internal order, decision-making procedures, communication channels, and power centers, must be maintained. Whenever there is stress and strain in these areas, action is necessary to maintain output at a satisfactory level. In this regard there is equifinality of functioning; that is, the initial conditions of the system do not completely determine its activities or its final state, and it is possible for many courses of action to be followed in pursuit of the same outcome. Homeostasis depends on the continual flow of information into the system. Part of the output must be returned in the form of feedback information which can in turn be used to guide and control the future activities of the system. It is effective homeostasis action which gives overall stability and unity, or a steady state, to the system, and this helps it to survive.

5. *The process of morphogenesis is also assumed to be operating.* Morphogenesis is the process of developing which keeps the system moving toward order, complexity, adaptability, unity, and operational effectiveness. This does not mean that the system needs to move in all these directions at the same time. Neither does it mean that development in one area necessarily produces growth in all other areas. However, through the process of morphogenesis the system grows in complexity and internal ordering and in the ability to control its activities and achieve its goals. Development is achieved when there is a favorable enough ratio between input and output so that there is a surplus to devote to the growth of the system. Informational feedback, is the fundamental aspect of morphogenesis. The growth of a system does not always depend on rational thought or purposeful goal-achieving activity. Chance occurrences often benefit the system, and actions of which actors are not even aware sometimes contribute to development. [4]

6. *Tension is a normal structural condition of open systems.* Stress and strain are normal for an open system because no two actors ever place exactly the same interpretation on expectations. [5] An elaboration of the results of tension can be understood in terms of the antithesis of social organization and social disorganization. The latter process is characteristic of positive entropy, but may well result in reorganization at a higher level of efficiency.

II. THE STRUCTURAL ELEMENTS OF COMPLEX SYSTEMS OF SOCIAL ORGANIZATION

The structural elements of complex organization, which are used as the analytical units for the study made, are presented in this section. It may be noted that these elements are conceived of as the units which make up simple organizational units or groups, and that a complex organization is seen as a multi-group structure. [6]

The most detailed and systematic definitions known to this investigator, are found in the works of Frederick L. Bates. Bates has developed definitions for key concepts over a period of years. [7] His works make clear the kind of units which comprise units of social organization, as well as the kind of relationships which exist between these units.

As used in this work, the smallest analytical unit which relates an actor to a group is seen as a norm. A norm is identified as a single behaviorial expectation. [8] Sets of norms, which are organized around the performance of a function, are envisioned as roles. Roles are related to an actor. The next largest structural unit is the status position, which may be described as made up of the several roles played by a given actor. Status positions locate the actor in a group. Social groups are seen as made up of status positions, and a social group is defined as a social entity consisting of at least two individuals who interact with each other as the occupants of two positions, each of which contains at least one role reciprocal to a role in the other position. [9] A group is, furthermore, composed of all individuals who occupy positions reciprocal to all other positions in the same structure, and it contains no individuals who do not meet this requirement. [10]

The structural unit which is the focus of this study, complex social organization is made up of groups. A complex organization is deliberately formed by linking two or more groups in order to attain specific goals. [11]

It is in order at this point to follow through with an actor-related approach to social organizational analysis. In a complex organization an actor may occupy several positions, since he may be located in several of the component groups of the organization. The constellation of status positions, which are customarily occupied by a single actor or type of actor, is his situs. The prestige and power of the holder of a situs will normally be related to the number of positions which make it up. The larger the number of positions in a particular occupational situs, for example, the greater will be the prestige and power of the situs. The final actor-related concept used in this analysis is "station". The location of the actor in the total community or society is his station, which, in turn, is the total collection of his situses. [12] This concept is relevant to the analysis of a complex organization in that the most prestigious and powerful positions will likely be held by actors who occupy situses in several of the more important basic social systems of the community. In fact, the prestige and power of any complex organization which may be investigated can be determined empirically by the number and importance of the stations of all actors who are part of the organization.

All of the concepts treated in this chapter will be used in the analyses which follows. The various definitions were operationalized in the following manner for clarity and ready reference.

1. *Social organization* is the embodiment of norms in concrete social relations. Ways of acting, interacting, and thinking, which people who live together develop, give order to their behavior.

2. A *social system* is a plurality of individual actors interacting with each other in a situation which has at least a physical or environmental aspect, actors who are motivated in terms of a tendency to the optimization of gratification and whose relations in their situations, including each other, is defined and mediated in terms of a system of culturally structured and shared symbols over time.

3. An *open system* is a bounded set of interrelated activities that together constitute a single social system which is articulated by exchanges with its external environment.

4. A *norm* is a single behavioral expectation, or how one actor expects another to behave in a given instance.

5. A *role* is a set of related norms that is all the behavior which one actor expects from another which relates to a function or need both actors share.

6. A *status position* is the combination of the several roles which one actor plays in a group. It is the structural place of the actor.

7. A *situs* is the constellation of status positions held by one actor in one complex organization. Again, it is his structural place in this social unit.

8. A *station* is the total collection of situses which an actor holds. In other words, it is his structural place in a total community or society.
9. A *group* is a simple social system made up of two or more actors whose interaction forms a web of reciprocal role relations oriented to the attainment of a common goal.
10. A *complex organization* is a combination of two or more groups with specialized functions linked together into a single structure by reciprocal role relationships dedicated to a common goal.

III. A BEHAVIORAL MODEL AND THE INVESTIGATION OF SOCIAL DISORGANIZATION

In this last section the writer sets forth the model utilized in the organization of study findings. This model was designed to account for tensions involving stresses and strains, normal features of social systems. In this regard, it has already been stated that a college-type organization, especially a western-type educational-religious system in an eastern cultural setting, has built into its social structure specially high potentials for stress and strain. This is due to the diverse cultural backgrounds which characterize its actors. Furthermore, the fact that the outside culture is an important source of input (finance, equipment, tools, *et cetera*) necessitates strategies and actions which may be sources of friction within the system. These high stress factors are added to the normal tensions which occur in such organizations.

F. L. Bates and H. L. Nix, in the tradition of Sorokin, Parsons, Merton, and Robin Williams, have set forth in great clarity and detail a conceptual scheme which will be used as the behavioral model for this study. 13 The conceptual scheme followed provides a model for what may be called a "perfectly organized system". This model has the features of a general behavioral model, and is therefore useful in analyzing the structural features of a complex organization, such as is the subject of this study. Features of stress and strain in the model are not thought of as disorganization, except in the sense that tension and disorganization are normal to a healthy system. It is believed the model has special utility for a study which focuses on the survival strategies of a complex organization. This belief is based on the necessity:

1. to visualize a normative system for a complex educational-religious organization;

2. to articulate the strains which are the result to some extent of the western-type system functioning in an eastern cultural setting, and to show the role-stresses which they bring to the structure;
3. to isolate the mechanisms utilized to prevent strain in and possible entropy to the system, and finally
4. to indicate how the system was able to maintain homeostasis and some semblance of a steady state in its ever-recurring processes of maintenance and development.

The four independent variables (factors) which comprise the behavioral model used are defined and described below.

1. *The Cultural Structure.* All the learned and expected patterns of behavior which members of society share comprise the cultural structure. Culture is made up of customs, or overt behavior expectations, values or emotionally-laid behavior expectations, and beliefs or intellectual behavior expectations. It has already been made clear that no two actors are socialized, and thus internalize norms, in the same way. These sources of structural differences are always present, and they often result in deviance. The latter is known and identified by such terms as cultural lag, cultural relativity, cultural shock, and cultural conflict. Deviance results in disorganizational processes which in turn trigger organizational processes of feedback and entropy. In all cultures, and certainly in the eastern setting of this study, the range of tolerable deviance is usually quite wide. In other words, there is a permissiveness in the structure which permits a range of behavior.

2. *Personality.* The personality is understood to be made up of all the biological attributes, including age, sex, and race, and all the psychological attributes, including capacities, drives, ideas, attitudes, and habits which characterize an individual. With the possibility of varieties of combinations of these attributes in the Chinese and western actors who are part of the organizational structure of this study, one can readily see the likelihood of differences in self-images and personality. Personality styles are brought to this social unit, and continue to be maintained more or less, although a socialization process begins immediately.

3. *The Situation.* The social situation has to do with all the conditions, including the social and physical environment, which set limits for and influences activity. The social environment has to do with the number and the kind of social units an individual actor has contacts with or in, as well as the social settings

for these contacts. The Hong Kong physical and social environment in general, and the particular physical and social circumstances of the Hong Kong Baptist College and its actors, set the limits for and influence the activity of the individuals under study. The position taken is that the situation will be by each actor defined in terms of his cultural background and his personality.

4. *Social Interaction.* Concrete interaction emerges on the basis first of what actors recognize to be the ideal or expected behavior and then translated through their personality structure and definition of the situation. Thus, interaction becomes the intervening variable in the form of social control and communication which bring cultural structure, personality, and situation together. [14]

Utilization of the above behavioral model makes it possible to identify role stresses pertinent to the study made. These stresses have been classified as follows: [15]

1. *Maladjustment within the cultural structure itself.* If stress arises from a condition in which the players of roles perceive that they are confronted with incompatible norms either as felt obligations or perceived pressures, the stress is called *role conflict*. If such attributes as rewards, prestige, authority, and functional importance associated with a role are out of balance with one another or internally inconsistent, the stress is called *role incongruity.*

2. *Maladjustment between the cultural structure and personality.* When actors or classes of actors are unable to fulfill their perceived roles the resultant deviance is said to be the result of *role inadequacy*. A stratification system may allocate persons with less than the necessary abilities to gain access to certain roles, or the socialization process may fail to provide a large enough number of individuals to fill role vacancies. Either eventuality will result in incapacity (biological or psychological) to play required roles.

3. *Maladjustment between the cultural structure and a situation.* When a significant number of actors or a class of actors fail to fulfill a perceived role because of repetitive situational factors, the result is referred to as *role frustration*. Inadequacies in the situation or inconsistency between role expectation and the social and physical reality in this case blocks role performance.

4. *Maladjustment between the cultural structure and social interaction.* If stress arises in connection with interaction, it may be termed *role non-reciprocity*. In such an example, one actor fails to react to another.

In the body of the analysis the normal state of the organizational structure will be conceived of as:

1. a condition of freedom from conflict between roles or within the contents
    of roles;
2. a situation in which members of the organization can perform their roles
    without suffering stress as a result;
3. a situation in which all the necessary conditions for role performance are
    supplied;
4. a situation in which all the roles are related to each other in such a way
    that when interaction takes place the behavior of the actors is reciprocal
    and complementary.

This will set the stage for the articulation of the stresses which are classified
above. It will also provide a background for the presentation of the mechanisms,
or survival strategies, which the actors in the Hong Kong Baptist College have
used to provide for its maintenance and development.

---

1. Walter Buckley, *Sociology and Modern Systems Theory* (Englewood Cliffs, New
Jersey: Prentice-Hall, Inc., 1967).

2. *Ibid.*, p. 82.

3. Daniel Katz and Robert L. Kahn, *The Social Psychology of Organization* (New
York: John Wiley and Sons, 1966), pp. 19-26.

4. Marvin E. Olsen, *The Process of Social Organization* (New York: Holt, Rinehart,
and Winston, 1968), pp. 229-34.

5. A. L. Bertrand, *Basic Sociology: An Introduction to Theory and Method* (New
York: Appleton-Century-Crofts, 1967), pp. 1-7.

6. Talcott Parsons, *Structure and Process in Modern Societies* (Glencoe, Illinois:
The Free Press, 1960), p. 56.

7. See "Position, Role, and Status: A Reformulation of Concepts," *Social Forces*,
Vol. 34, No. 4 (May, 1956), pp. 313-21; "A Conceptual Analysis of Group Structure,"
Social Forces, Vol. 35, No. 3 (1957), pp. 103-11; "Institutions, Organizations, and Com-
munities: A General Theory of Complex Structure," *The Pacific Sociological Review*,
Vol. 3, No. 2 (1960); *An Outline of Structural Concepts*, mimeographed (Baton Rouge:
Department of Sociology, Louisiana State University, December, 1968).

8. See Neal Gross, Ward S. Mason and Alexander W. McEachern, *Explorations in
Role Analysis* (New York: John Wiley and Sons, Inc., 1966), p. 60, where "an expectation"
is used in the same sense as a norm. For more detailed treatments of norms see Muzafer
Sherif, *The Psychology of Social Norms* (New York: Harper and Brothers Publishers, 1936),
and Rangor Rommetveit, *Social Norms and Roles* (Minneapolis, Minnesota: University of
Minnesota Press, 1955).

9. *Ibid.*, p. 48. Also, see A. L. Bertrand, "A Structural Analysis of Differential Patterns of Social Relations, A Role Theory Perspective for Rural Sociology," a Presidential address delivered at the 1968 annual meeting of the Rural Sociology Society, Boston, Massachusetts, August, 1968.

10. Frederick L. Bates, "A Conceptual Analysis of Group Structures," *Social Forces*, Vol. 35, No. 3 (1957), pp. 103-11.

11. Frederick L. Bates, "Institutions, Organizations, and Communities: A General Theory of Complex Structures," *Pacific Sociological Review*, Vol. 3, No. 2 (1960).

12. Frederick L. Bates, *An Outline of Structural Concepts*, mimeographed (Baton Rouge: Department of Sociology, Louisiana State University, December, 1968).

13. F. L. Bates and H. L. Nix, "Social Disorganization of the Group Level: A Role Theory Approach," *United College Journal*, (Hong Kong), Vol. 3 (1964). The main concepts used and explained in this work are utilized in developing the behavioral model of this study.

14. See F. L. Bates and H. L. Nix, *op. cit.*

15. Harold L. Nix and Frederick L. Bates, "Occupational Role Stress: A Structural Approach," *Rural Sociology*, Vol. 27, No. 1 (March, 1962), pp. 7-17.

CHAPTER IV

METHODOLOGICAL TECHNIQUES
AND APPROACHES

The present research, as stated previously, represents an exploratory effort to use a system model combined with a behavioral model for a new conceptual approach to analyze the structural components of a western-type college organization in an eastern culture. The focus of the analysis is upon the survival strategies and related behavior of Chinese and western occupants of relevant status positions in the structure of the Hong Kong Baptist College. The purpose of this chapter is to describe the techniques employed in data collection and to mention some of the problems encountered in their use.

The primary techniques of data collection were participant observation and the use of records, communications, informants, personal documents, interviews, and questionnaires. This follows the traditional pattern of sociologists who in case-studies have collected and used both qualitative and quantitative materials. [1]   The pattern in this study has been to interweave quantitative data, obtained from interviews and questionnaires used originally for other purposes, with the material from sources such as records of group meetings, statistical and other school reports, and organizational and public communications, and general observation and information about the cultural setting. Some of the advantages and shortcomings of these instruments, and the problems encountered in their use, are given.

THE PARTICIPANT OBSERVER ROLE

The writer first gained experience in working with Oriental people in organizational settings in Hawaii, where his major assignment was to administer a school attended mainly by students of Japanese and Chinese ethnic origins. Later, in Canton, China, he spent two years in intensive study of the Cantonese dialect, and had an opportunity to learn the culture of the people through participation in conversations, and through formal and informal meetings with Chinese students and educational and church leaders. Still later, in Hong Kong, he spent several years in organizational positions and became familiar with Hong Kong cultural and social conditions in general, and with the local religious and educational aspects of culture in particular.

The experiences referred to above made possible the writer's appointment to an administrative and teaching position in the Hong Kong Baptist College, which he has held from its founding in 1956 to the present. By becoming a normal part of the organizational structure the writer has been able to share in the activities and sentiments of others and engage in many face-to-face relationships. This afforded opportunities to catch interactional processes as they occurred and to observe the perceptions of people playing reciprocal roles. Authorities in the field of research methods have pointed out how sympathetic identification and role-taking in the life of those observed makes possible meaningful analysis in working with one's data. [2]

However, there were disadvantages in such participant observation. Because of involvement and identification with other role-bearers it is next to impossible to constantly maintain an attitude of interested curiosity and matter-of-fact inquiry so important for scientific inquiry. The fact that the writer recognized that he as a westerner was not fully accepted by his fellow Chinese role-bearers tended to moderate his identification. He was treated by the Government of Hong Kong as a visitor, although a permanent one, and the Chinese, as well as the writer, recognized that some day he would leave permanently. This fact, perhaps made for less bias in the analysis. It lessened temptations to moralize and to make personal judgments. [3]

A difficult problem arose in the selection of meaningful material for analysis from among so much data available. The conceptual scheme employed and the analytical concepts used were helpful and necessary in the process of selection. [4]

THE USE OF RECORDS AND STATISTICAL REPORTS

Observation was supplemented by the use of records and statistical reports. Such material was especially useful in viewing trends over time and in assembling factual data for analysis and recording. [5]

The writer was constantly on the alert for inaccuracies in records used. Reports of a formal nature to other organizations in the community, and public communications, are especially subject to errors, as are reports of officials to their superiors. An effort to please a superior, or to enhance the organizational image, is often detected in such reporting. Furthermore, most records of group meetings show little of the interaction so important for meaningful analysis. The disagreements and strategies which come out in interaction and make up so much of group behavior are often covered up. [6]   In this particular investigation the presence of the researcher and his participation in most of the meetings made it possible for him to fill in from memory the interactions which took place, even though much of sentiments and meanings were not recorded. In this regard, it is readily admitted that memory is selective. No doubt many meanings and sentiments were only partially recalled, and the recall which came to the participant observer likely would be different in some detail from that which might come to other actors in the situation. [7]   It is hoped this type of bias was minimized in that the records of persons present and actions taken assisted in framing recall.

Such documents as annual catalogues and student yearbooks, as well as news bulletins, published by the school, and publicity materials for newspaper and magazine use, were utilized in the analysis. These materials reflect the broader aspects of the social climate at given time intervals and, because of their intentions to inform, amuse, and influence, are especially useful in a study which focuses on the survival strategies of a particular organization. These documents are not as reliable as statistical records and reports in the assembling of factual information, because they take on many qualities of propaganda. [8]

THE USE OF REPORTS OF INFORMANTS

When the writer could not attend certain meetings, he often asked for a report or received unsolicited information from persons present. Such reporting of interaction of behavior at formal meetings, and at informal meetings often unknown to the writer, was valuable. In some instances the motivation of the informant was suspect, especially when he was Chinese and held a position in the hierarchy lower than the position of the writer. Because of this, it was a practice of the writer to treat such reporters as true representatives of others only when they reported on matters well known to the group as a whole. In all cases the writer took into account that selective memory, mental sets, and personal bias likely colored such reports. They were useful, however, in staking out problem areas in organizational interaction and structure. [9]

THE USE OF PERSONAL DOCUMENTS

Life histories in the form of biograms, helped the writer understand the family background and the daily conditions under which many informants lived. Insights into behavior expectations and values were gleaned from these documents. The same was true of "spoken autobiographies" and "passive interviews." The latter were mainly useful in understanding the personalities of the persons involved and as background material for understanding and analysis of interaction patterns. [10] Furthermore, especially during periods of extended absence from Hong Kong in 1958-59, 1964-65, and 1968-69 letters from many staff members and some students were useful in understanding individual perceptions of stress situations.

THE USE OF INTERVIEWS AND QUESTIONNAIRES

Aside from the "passive interviews" referred to above, the writer had available recorded responses to structured interviews administered to respondents at various levels in the Hong Kong Baptist College's organizational structure. He also had the responses of student and faculty members to structured questionnaires administered to them. Responses, especially in questionnaires to students, provided considerable information as to social characteristics, which could be analyzed. However, since the specific formulation of the research problem came later, this material was useful only in secondary analysis, as is true of the records and other documents previously referred to.

The economic advantages of secondary analysis is well established. Material is available in great quantity and for a wide range of important problems.

The periodic nature of much of the information collected also is advantageous, especially in an organizational study which focuses on strategies used over a period of several years. [11]

Limitations in secondary analysis are likewise obvious. The operational definitions of the data were out of the researcher's control. There were no possibilities for experimental manipulation, since the data was not originally collected for the specific purposes of this study. [12] However, flexibility with respect to the form in which research questions are asked, and formulation of the research idea so that available material bears on the question, have made the use of secondary analysis a useful tool. [13]

CHRONOLOGICAL STAGES OF DATA COLLECTION

The decision to undertake this study was made by the writer in 1964. By then the Hong Kong Baptist College had developed some status as a senior college in the educational system of Hong Kong. Its permanent campus was in the process of being built. Data collection was done in several stages as shown below.

1. *Initial stage.* The assembling of administrative correspondence, of records of meetings, of catalogues, yearbooks, newssheets and articles in newspapers was begun immediately. A bilingual questionnaire, pretested with Senior sociology students in the college was administered to over ninety percent of the student-body during the 1963-64 session. This provided data on their social characteristics and their attitudes and opinions on selected subjects.

2. *Intermediate procedures.* In the autumn of 1965 the investigator began in earnest the process of participant observation for this research. He also assembled other materials. At this time he was serving as one of the administrators of the college. During this period he selected and organized materials from such documents as the minutes of the Hong Kong-Macau Baptist Mission, the Baptist Association, and government publications related to education. He copied select data from the various offices of the college. He assembled materials about the faculty and staff of the college. He helped administer a questionnaire to the faculty and staff in 1966 from which the social characteristics and attitudes and opinions on important educational issues of the faculty and staff could be analyzed. He discussed college matters in a normal regular way with administrators, teachers and students, as part of his day-by-day activity. He had access to re-

sponses of certain administrators, faculty, and students in an open-end structured interview conducted by a team of researchers who came to Hong Kong to make a special study of church-related organizations for Higher Education in the Colony. The tabulated results of a questionnaire administered by the faculty in the English Department, in 1966, to get student reaction to the methods of teaching and felt problems in the department were available for use. He also personally administered a questionnaire, in 1966, to the freshmen students with the purpose of comparing the social characteristics of this entering class, by departments.

3. *The completion of the process.* In the Fall of 1968 the investigator administered a revised version of the questionnaire used in 1964 to over two-thirds of the 1968-69 student body. He and a number of helpers systematically gathered and tabulated additional data, such as the activities centered around religious-emphasis week in 1968, the characteristics of students who are office-holders in student organizations and students who perform special functions in the school, and the characteristics of college graduates. He coded the information from these questionnaires and supervised the punching of IBM cards for machine tabulation of data from these investigations.

---

1. Emile Durkheim, *The Division of Labor in Society,* translated by George Simpson (Glencoe, Illinois: The Free Press, 1947), pp. 34-38, was one of the early social theorists who commented on the use of observation in research. He saw scientific method, as (1) the careful observation, description, and classification of facts, followed by (2) discovery in them of an ordering principle related to causes.

Durkheim also analysed statistical data collected for purposes other than those of his particular study. See *Suicide,* translated by George Simpson (Glencoe, Illinois: Free Press, 1951).

Field study as a method was, perhaps, most widely used by anthropologists in the study of primitive societies at first. B. Malinowski's *Crime and Custom in Savage Society* (New York: Harcourt, Brace and Company, 1926), is an example of an anthropological functional analysis of the type referred to. A well-known sociological application of the anthropological approach is found in the Lynd's study of Middletown. See Robert S. Lynd and Helen Merrell Lynd, *Middletown* (New York: Harcourt, Brace and Company, 1929). They employed participant observation, along with a thorough examination of as many documentary materials as were available. To this they added informal interviewing and written questionnaires as well. Thus, they went beyond the traditional anthropological method by using quantitative techniques to supplement their qualitative materials. This pattern of utilizing in a single case-study both qualitative and quantitative data has often been used by other social scientists. Examples are: W. Lloyd Warner, *Yankee City* (New Haven: Yale University Press, 1963); William Whyte, *Street Corner Society* (Chicago: University of Chicago Press, 1955); Arthur J. Vidich and Joseph Bensman, *Small Town in*

Mass Society (Princeton: Princeton University Press, 1958); Morris Schwartz, *The Nurse and the Mental Patient* (New York: Russell Sage Foundation, 1956); Howard Becker, *Boys in White* (Chicago: University of Chicago Press, 1961); and A.B. Hollingshead, *Elmtown's Youth* (New York: John Wiley and Sons, 1949); Joseph H. Fichter, S.J., *Social Relations in the Urban Parish* (Chicago: University of Chicago Press, 1954); F.J. Roethlisberger and W.J. Dickson, *Management and the Worker* (Cambridge: Harvard University Press, 1943).

The well-known research of W.I. Thomas and Florian Znaniecki, *The Polish Peasant in Europe and America* (New York: Dover Publications, 1958), which investigated social and personal disorganization and reorganization, relied on expressive personal documents, mainly series of letters coupled with observation, for analysis. The letters supplemented previous knowledge of Polish society by observation especially of Znaniecki, and observation of the Polish community in the United States. Perhaps, no other case-study has used personal documents as extensively as they. The many discussions as to the scientific value of this work, including the critique of Herbert Blumer: *An Appraisal of Thomas and Znaniecki's "The Polish Peasant in Europe and America,"* (New York: Social Science Research Council, 1939) have called attention to and criticized their extensive use of personal documents. However, since personal documents did not feature largely in this particular study, these criticisms will not be pursued further. However, some students of Robert Park and Ernest Burgess, who followed in the Thomas and Znaniecki tradition with similar but less ambitious studies, are here listed: Clifford Shaw, *Brothers in Crime* (Chicago: The University of Chicago Press, 1938); Frederick Thrasher, *The Gang* (Chicago: The University of Chicago Press, 1927); L. Wirth, *The Ghetto* (Chicago: The University of Chicago Press, 1956); P.V. Young, *Pilgrims of Russian-town* (New York: Russell and Russell, 1967); and Harvey Zorbaugh, *Gold Coast and the Slum* (Chicago: The University of Chicago Press, 1929). These and other similar well-known works attest to the usefulness and adaptability of participant observation and varied uses of documents in case-study research.

2. See Severyn T. Bruyn, *The Human Perspective in Sociology: The Methodology of Participant Observation* (Englewood Cliffs, New Jersey: Prentice-Hall, Inc., 1966), pp. 12-14, 188; Leon Festinger and Daniel Katz, *Research Methods in the Behavioral Sciences* (New York: Holt, Rinehart, and Winston, 1953), pp. 71-72; Norris S. Schwartz and Charlotte G. Schwartz, "Problems in Participant Observation," *American Journal of Sociology*, Vol. 60 (January, 1955), pp. 350-51; and W. Richard Scott, "Field Methods in the Study of Organization," James G. March, editor, *Handbook of Organizations* (Chicago: Rand McNelly and Company, 1965), pp. 286-87.

3. Norris S. Schwartz and Charlotte G. Schwartz, *Ibid.*, pp. 350-51, point out that personal involvement and scientific attitude are not necessarily mutually exclusive.

4. See W. Richard Scott, *op. cit.*, pp. 286-87.

5. Claire Selltiz, and others, *Research Methods in Social Relations* (New York: Holt, Rinehart, and Winston, Inc., 1959) pp. 201, 316 state that in organizational studies such materials supplement observation by helping to establish trends over time and in verifying factual material brought into an analysis. Burton R. Clark, *The Open Door College: A Case Study* (New York: McGraw-Hill Book Company, Inc., 1960), p. 181, comments on the usefulness of minutes of group meetings and field records in the study of a school system.

6. *Ibid.*, p. 323, and R. C. Angell and R. Freedman, "The Use of Documents, Records, and Census Materials and Indices," L. Festinger and D. Katz, editors, *Research Methods in the Behavioral Sciences* (New York: Dryden Press, 1953), pp. 300-26.

7. W. Richard Scott, *op. cit.*, p. 285.

8. Selltiz, *op. cit.*, pp. 330-42.

9. *Ibid.*, pp. 291-93.

10. Robert C. Angell and Ronald Freedman, *op. cit.*, pp. 303-5, refer to the value of such expressive documents in becoming generally acquainted with a culture or sub-culture. Since such documents are used in this study only for this purpose, it does not seem necessary to review the literature further. See pp. 306-9 for difficulties encountered in using such documents for scientific verification.

11. Robert C. Angell and Ronald Freedman, *op. cit.*, pp. 310-16; and Selltiz, *et al.*, *op. cit.*, pp. 316-22.

12. *Ibid.*, pp. 322-23.

13. *Ibid.*, pp. 317-19. The authors here call attention to the skillful way Emile Durkheim's well-known Suicide study, although dependent on analysis of data collected for other purposes, was used to test a social theory.

CHAPTER V

THE STUDY SETTING:
MODERN HONG KONG AND
ITS PEOPLE

Hong Kong is a Crown Colony of approximately 400 square miles. The first part of what now constitutes the Colony was ceded to Great Britain by China in 1842. This cession was part of the Treaty of Nanking, which brought to an end what is sometimes called the Opium War. A second portion of Hong Kong was ceded to Britain in 1860 as a part of the Treaty of Peking in which China surrendered more rights and territory to several European powers. The largest portion of the Colony, known as the New Territories, was leased by England in 1898. This lease is to run out in 1997.

Hong Kong developed as a trading center during the nineteenth century. During the same time the nearby Chinese empire, under the Manchu dynasty, began to crumble. [1] The Manchu empire finally collapsed in 1911, and Republic of China was established under the leadership of Dr. Sun Yat Sen. Dr. Sun had lived in the Colony and attended the University of Hong Kong, while in disfavor in China. Sun Yat Sen died in 1928. At his death Chiang Kai-shek became the head of a government which was harassed by the growing military power of Japan. This harassment was followed by Japanese occupation of parts of South China and of Hong Kong in the early 1940's. This occupation was not lifted until the end of the World War II in 1945. A short period of rebuilding in both Hong Kong and China was interrupted in 1949 by Communist political success. The history of the Colony since that time is of special interest to this study.

Demographic Characteristics

The population of Hong Kong was estimated to be 1,857,000 in 1949. Since that time it has grown rapidly through migration from China and natural increase. The Hong Kong census of 1961 indicated that there were 3,184,000 persons living in the Colony at that time. [2]   Today (1969) the population of Hong Kong is estimated to be about 4,000,000, and it is expected to reach 6,000,000 by 1981. [3]

Approximately one million people have migrated from China to Hong Kong since the Second World War. This migration occurred primarily in four distinct periods of heavy movement as follows: (1) 1945 to 1947, when many former residents returned to the Colony following the defeat of the Japanese; (2) 1949-50, when there was huge influx of refugees with the change over of a administration in China; (3) 1957-58, when another wave of refugees arrived from China, and finally (4) 1961-1963 when a huge wave of refugees broke through the land borders of Hong Kong. [4]   This heavy migration boosted population growth from a natural rate of about three percent to an actual rate of five percent over the entire post war period. [5]   Barring other unforseen migrations to Hong Kong from China, the rate of population growth in the decades ahead is projected at three percent. [6]

Comparisons of the Census of 1931 and of 1961 show that significant changes took place in the age and sex structure of the people of the Colony. At the earlier period the percentage of persons under 15 was considerably less than in 1961, while the percentage of persons over 60 was less. This age distribution was due primarily to the transient nature of the population in 1931. Furthermore, in 1931 the census showed a sex ratio of three men to two women, indicating the selectiveness of male migration at this earlier period. By 1961, 41 percent of the population was under 15 years of age as compared to 27 percent in 1931; 4.8 percent was over 60, compared to 3.6 in 1931; and 54 percent were between 15 and 60, compared to 69 percent in 1931. Thus, the age structure of the Colony had become more like that of a permanent population. In this regard, although the population was still 5 percent more male than female, the trend was toward a more normal sex distribution. [7]

Economic Characteristics

The phenomenal economic growth of Hong Kong during the last two decades has been called a miracle. This growth is attributed to a change from an entrepot center serving China to an industrialized economy. Previous to 1960, trading volume was two to three times that of the industrial output of the Colony. Currently, that trading activity amounts to only one and one-half times the gross domestic product. Despite this change, international trade is still a leading factor in the economic growth of Hong Kong. The noticeable change is the import of raw materials for industrial fabrication in Hong Kong and export of manufactured products to world markets. [8]

The migration of one million people to Hong Kong since the Second World War had a profound effect on its economy. This migration provided the hugh influx of capital, management, and labor necessary for the change-over to an industrial economy. From 1955 to 1965 the growth in band deposits in Hong Kong was more than sixfold. [9] At the same time savings and fixed deposits increased fifteen-fold. [10] A large number of professional and technical persons among the refugees to the Colony provided manpower at the managerial levels needed for industry. [11] The wave of migration was also especially selective for ages 20-29, the ages needed to supply an industrial labor force. [12]

Foreign investments from non-Chinese sources became a predominant factor in the growth of new industries. By 1965 there were 541 foreign companies registered in the Colony. The United States, Great Britain and Japan each contributed more than one billion Hong Kong dollars in total investments in a short period of time. [13]

Projections indicate the trend toward increased industrialization is continuing. However, the writer has no concrete evidence to support this belief. The bank crisis which occurred in 1965 and the leftist disturbances in 1966-67 noticeably interrupted and adversely affected economic developments. Currently, the situation is being stabilized and the economy appears healthy again. [14] One clue to the economic progress of Hong Kong is found in the growing affluence of its citizens. The net annual income per person in Hong Kong had reached U.S.$400.00 by 1964. This is quite high by Asian Standards. [15] As late as 1948, per capita income was less than U.S.$200.00. [16] In the early 1950's the empoverished refugee population was assisted by many private and governmental organizations. However, by the end of the 1960's the welfare needs had become those expected of a settled community.

TABLE I
HONG KONG
EMPLOYMENT STRUCTURE, 1961 AND 1965 (PROJECTION)

Type of Employment	1961		1965	
	Number	Percent	Number	Percent
Primary Production	96,000	8.1	96,000	6.0
Manufacturing	476,000	39.9	732,000	45.8
Building and construction	100,000	8.4	172,000	10.8
Services	502,000	42.2	598,000	37.4
Unclassified	17,000	1.4	---	---
TOTALS	1,191,000	100.0	1,598,000	100.0

A reconstructed summary of Table IX, pp. 34-35 of K.R. Chou in *The Hong Kong Economy* (Hong Kong: Economic Research Centre, The Chinese University of Hong Kong, 1966).

Cultural Characteristics

To understand the Chinese people of present day Hong Kong, it is necessary to understand their cultural background. Ideologically, Chinese social structure is built on the humanistic philosophy of Confucius. An ordinary Chinese child learns about Confucius as early as an American child in a Christian family learns about Jesus Christ. The "Four Books" of Confucius are read in primary school, and the history, philosophy, and literature of China are taught as major subjects, throughout secondary school and in college. Those who do not go to school or attend English schools, are socialized in families in which Confucian teaching, i.e., filial piety, propriety, human heartedness, "the golden mean," permeate thought and action. All Hong Kong Chinese hear Confucian ideas discussed and learn them as a part of their indoctrination into the rules of their society. Confucianism has traditionally dominated social relationships, and along with veneration of ancestors and avoidance of evil spirits, is evident in most day-to-day relationships.

The above is not to say that Confucian-based political order has not changed. Apparently, both in China and in Hong Kong the traditional social order is deteriorating rather rapidly. However, the familial structure, based on Confucian filial piety, continues to survive. All in all, the spirit of Confucianism still has a great influence on the average Hong Kong residents' conceptions of the universe. [17]

Most Hong Kong families live as small conjugal rather than as extended family units. Nonetheless, filial bonds are reinforced thorugh traditional festivals, especially the Chinese New Year celebrations, and customs related to marriage, birth, and death going back to traditional times. The family, the clan, and the native-place mutual-aid, and other, societies play an important role in social life and activities.

The average Hong Kong Chinese views the universe as in a transitional process, circular in movement and not necessarily moving toward some absolutely completed and finished end. He does not necessarily hold to the concept of a divine power in control. Such a cosmic view and attitude, can be seen in the modern Chinese's conception of the world as basically good and his enjoyment of food and material things.

The Christian church, western-type education, and western secular influences have clashed with many of the beliefs which formerly upheld the traditional Chinese social order. The majority in Hong Kong appear to have adopted to the corroding western influences which have challenged the traditional values and ways by short-term expedients. That is, they have adopted many material innovations and some non-material cultural values of the West to cope with the new situations in which they find themselves. However, the deep conflicts in the differing ideologies probably are far from being reconciled, by the average person. [18] Familial solidarity and traditional values continue to be reinforced in many ways. Weddings, births, and funerals require traditional rites for the great majority who have not embraced Christianity. Ancient Animistic religious practices, overlaid with Taoist and Buddhist religious beliefs and rites, are still in evidence everywhere.

Educational Characteristics

Much effort has been put forth by the Hong Kong government to improve and extend the educational needs of a rapidly growing population. In 1946, at the end of the Japanese occupation, there were less than 60,000 students at all levels in schools in the Colony. [19] With the return of British control, the number in school jumped to 331,000 by 1957. [20] It was estimated at that time that there were between 400,000 and 500,000 school-aged young people in a population of two and one-half million.

The last two decades have witnessed the erection of many new schools and increasing study opportunities for students. For example, during the 1964-65 session a total of 866,120 students at all levels, from pre-primary to university, were reported as enrolled in institutions of learning as follows:

	TOTAL	MALE	FEMALE
Pre-primary	45,494	27,746	20,748
Primary	604,648	323,659	280,989
Secondary	172,918	99,957	72,961
Post-secondary	40,406	24,990	15,416
University	3,635	2,359	1,276
GRAND TOTAL	867,101 [21]	475,711	391,390

Analysis of the above enrollment figures shows that more than 54 percentage of students enrolled in pre-primary study were males. Also, almost 53 percent of the students in primary schools were males. At the secondary level 58 percent were males and 42 percent females. Of the students in post-secondary study, 62 percent were males and 38 percent females, while at the two universities 60 percent of the enrollees were males and 40 percent females.

At the pre-primary and primary levels, about nine out of ten students were in Chinese language schools. At the secondary level two out of three students were in schools where the chief medium of instruction was English. [22] At the post-secondary and university levels study secondary and university levels study is bilingual, with increasing emphasis on English as the medium of instruction. The pattern is for children to receive their primary education through the medium of Chinese, and to switch to an English-language school for secondary training. However, those who remain in Chinese language schools take English as a major subject and must be bilingual for college or university training.

It can be seen that, at the upper levels, boys are in a more favorable position than girls for educational opportunity. This is in line with the traditional views of Chinese, who place higher value on educating boys than girls.

Most schools are privately operated, but many are government-assisted and have varied types of government control. Tuition is low in the government-aided schools, but high in the private or partially subsidized ones. The aim, which has not yet been achieved is primary educational opportunity for all.

Private schools have varying standards, and can be classified from very poor to excellent. At the primary and secondary levels of education the government controls the final examinations. Syllabi are issued to guide teachers and students in preparating the latter for examinations. A certificate, issued on successful completion of the government examination, is necessary to advance from primary to secondary education in government and most government-aided secondary schools. Similarly, a certificate issued at the completion of secondary study is required for entrance in university-preparatory courses of one or two years' duration, and to admission to teacher training or government-operated technical colleges.

Education beyond middle school is referred to in Hong Kong as either post-secondary or university. Middle school study is either in English or Chinese as the chief medium of instruction. Diplomas are issued at the end of Form 5 (the eleventh grade in the United States).

A student who intends to matriculate in the English-language University of Hong Kong (established early in the twentieth century) must complete two additional years in an English-language middle school before he is eligible to sit for the University entrance examination. A student who intends to matriculate in the Chinese University of Hong Kong (founded in 1963) [23] must complete one additional year in either a Chinese or English-language middle school before he is eligible to sit for the Chinese University entrance examination. [24] Post-secondary colleges, such as Technical and Teacher Training Government-operated schools, allow properly certified middle school graduates, to sit for their entrance examinations.

A dozen or more private post-secondary colleges, of which the Hong Kong Baptist College is one, admit graduates of either English-language or Chinese-language middle schools for study. Such students pursue either four or five years of study, after which they are issued diplomas, equivalent more or less to the bachelor degrees given in the United States.

The Hong Kong Baptist College expects to be registered (in 1969) under a government post-secondary ordinance. When achieved this will, by definition, mean that the standard of the school is equivalent to or approaching that of a University College. It is the only post-secondary college which has applied for this status in Hong Kong.

1. A. Waley, *The Opium War Through Chinese Eyes* (London: Allen and Unwin, 1958); Li Chien Nung, *The Political History of China*, 1840-1928 (New York: Van Nostrand, 1963); and G.B. Endicott, *A History of Hong Kong* (Oxford University Press, 1964).

2. The Hong Kong Census, 1961 (Hong Kong: Government Printing Press, 1962

3. R.F. Simpson, *Problems of Education Planning in Hong Kong* (Hong Kong: Hong Kong Council of Education Research, 1966), p. 12.

4. K.R. Chow, *The Hong Kong Economy* (Hong Kong: Economic Research Centre, The Chinese University of Hong Kong, 1966), pp. 11-13.

5. *Ibid.*, p. 4.

6. *Ibid.*, pp. 14-17.

7. *Ibid.*, pp. 15-16.

8. *Ibid.*, pp. 36-43.

9. *Ibid.*, p. 64.

10. *Ibid.*, p. 64.

11. *Ibid.*, pp. 4-5.

12. *Ibid.*, p. 25.

13. *Ibid.*, pp. 77-78.

14. *The Hong Kong Report, 1968* (Hong Kong, Government Press, 1969), The Section on Industry.

15. K.R. Chow, *op. cit.*, p. 8.

16. *Ibid.*, p. 84, Table XXVII.

17. See Ch'u Chai and Winberg Chai, *The Changing Society of China* (New York: The New American Library of World Literature, Inc., 1962), pp. 66-80; F.S.C. Northrop, *Meeting of the East and West*, 2nd edition, (New York: Collier-Macmillan Company, 1966), pp. 419-423; Don Martindale, *Social Life and Cultural Change* (New York: D. Van Nostrand Company, Inc., 1962), pp. 135-61. It is difficult to say about the people of China except that the refugees to Hong Kong still give evidence of Confucian orientation.

18. See Michael G. Whisson, *Under the Rug* (Hong Kong: The South China Morning Post, Ltd., 1965), pp. 29-33 for a more pessimistic view regarding the eroding effects of western influences. Franklin Frazier, Race and Culture Contacts in the Modern World (Boston: Beacon Press, 1957), pp. 306-19, also discusses the role of missionaries and educators as agents of western civilization in Asian and African cultural areas, and suggests that they are contributing to the making of marginal men. F.S.C. Northrop, *op. cit.*, pp. 417-19, comments on the effects of western missionaries and educators who have influenced epople to give up their "intuitively and aesthetically grounded religion of emotion and other cultural forms for western religious and other cultural forms." The result, he says, has been the taking on of western traits and values, including western aggressiveness, which to the Orientals was especially noticeable.

19. S.H. Pang, *The Needs of Hong Kong, 1957*, a presentation to the constitution on world needs and strategy. A mimeographed paper (Les Rasses, Switzerland, May, 1958), p.4.

20. *Hong Kong Annual Report, 1957* (Hong Kong: Government Press, 1958), p. 131.

21. R.F. Simpson, *op. cit.*, Appendix A.

22. *Ibid.*, Appendix A.

23. Three private post-secondary schools, Chung Chi, New Asia, and United, became the foundation colleges of a federated-type government-supported University. These three colleges were founded in the early 1950's, just prior to the opening of the Hong Kong Baptist College in 1956, and were successful in gaining government support in 1959. They had formed a Joint Council in 1957 with the intention of coordinating entrance examina-

tions, curricula, and efforts to achieve government support and eventual university status. The Hong Kong Baptist College had maintained close fraternal relations with the colleges and their Joint Council but had not sought membership in the council for a variety of reasons. It sought to gain admission as a privately-supported college to the Chinese University, but failed for a number of reasons. Chief among the reasons given was the government-policy to admit colleges which were willing to accept government financial support and subsequent stricter government control.

24. The bachelor's degree at the University of Hong Kong is normally conferred after the successful completion of three years of study. Except for Oriental studies the medium of instruction is English. The bachelor's degree at the Chinese University of Hong Kong is conferred after the successful completion of four years of study. The media of instruction are Chinese and English. English-language middle school graduates, who complete one year of pre-university training, are eligible to sit for the Chinese University entrance examination, and may matriculate as first year students if examinations in Chinese are passed at an acceptable level. Both universities require adequate English proficiency for admission to study.

CHAPTER VI

PRELIMINARY STRATEGIES OF ORGANIZATION: THE FOUNDING OF THE HONG KONG BAPTIST COLLEGE

INTRODUCTION

The modern systems model outlined in Chapter IV provides a frame work for the conceptualization of the genesis of the Hong Kong Baptist College, which will be described and analyzed in this chapter in terms of strategies. These strategies may be envisioned as the actions taken by actors to achieve certain ends. Such behavior, together with the constraints which limited the range of alternate actions, can be seen as articulating a morphogenic process.

The material presented in this chapter is taken from records of one kind or another, as footnoted; or represents personal experience of the writer. Unless otherwise noted, accounts not footnoted represent participant-observation experiences.

The initial structural components of what became the Hong Kong Baptist College system were the few interacting individuals, all Chinese, who formed a group interested in founding a post-secondary college in Hong Kong. These individuals engaged in a conscious and deliberate purpose. Then were inspired by the following situational factors: (1) Mainland China had relatively recently been occupied by a Communist regime, and a million refugees, including students and educators, had settled in Hong Kong. (2) It was likely that the British Colony would have a period of relative stability and development. (3) More and more primary and secondary schools were being opened annually and several post-secondary Chinese-language colleges, had been established recently. (4) Organizations and agencies from the West, and their western personnel, were setting up headquarters in Hong Kong. Among them were missions formerly located in Mainland China, and missionaries, who served previously in China. (5) Hong Kong Christian and missionaries, who recently worked in China, were attuned to change. There had already begun an effort on a small scale, to strengthen and enlarge the Church and its units, and to establish and build up organizations, such as colleges, to serve the needs of the people.

The above mentioned Chinese actors were already linked with an Associational structure of Baptists through their membership in Baptist churches and their prior link with the Hong Kong-Macau Baptist Mission. The latter was an organization of Baptist Missionaries organized as a unit of the American Southern Baptist Foreign Mission Board. This set the stage for the first set of strategies employed. These actions and other strategies relating to the organization of Hong Kong Baptist College are described in the remainder of this chapter.

STRATEGIES DESIGNED TO DEVELOP A FORMAL ORGANIZATIONAL STRUCTURE

The above-mentioned individuals recognized the need for a formally organized and authorized group of Chinese Baptists and American missionaries to bring plans to completion. They made contacts with individuals in both groups whom they thought were most likely to be influential in the promotion of a college enterprise. The writer was among those contacted. This move was, in effect, the first of the several strategies to found the college. The second of these strategies was to get a formally constituted organizational committee.

The logical organization to form such a committee of Baptists was the association of all the Baptist churches in Hong Kong which had been constituted in 1938. It was known as the Hong Kong United Christian Baptist Churches Association. [1] This Association was legally incorporated in the Colony, and its members were authorized to hold and manage property on behalf of the churches, and to found and operate schools, hospitals, social centers, and the like.

It was recognized that the chairman of the Hong Kong Baptist Association was the key person to approach. He was a wealthy businessman, turned educator. He had a large family of successful sons and daughters. He was the most influential person in the largest Baptist church, as well as the principal of the Association-related Pui Ching Middle School. He owned a variety of banking, manufacturing, and commercial enterprises, and had had previous business connections in China. This man had just retired as the chairman of the Chinese YMCA. Having been born in the Swatow district of Kwong-tung Province in South China, he was a prominent member of this sub-group's association in Hong Kong. He had become a British subject by naturalization and was the recipient of the coveted title, O.B.E. (Officer of the British Empire). The latter was conferred by the Queen of England at special ceremonies which he attended in London. He had also just received an Honorary Doctorate from Oklahoma Baptist University. He was one of the officers of the Baptist World Alliance, representing Asia. In addition, this Chinese leader was especially hospitable to American and other Baptist leaders who visited Hong Kong, and to the missionaries there. He was not only in good standing with Protestant and Catholic Christians but with a large number of non-Christian community leaders and businessmen as well. [2]

The chairman of the Hong Kong Baptist Association was approached by a member of the informal group interested in a college. The latter had been selected for this role, because he was a protege of the chairman. The chairman was won over, and in turn placed the matter of college organizational committee on the agenda of 1954 annual meeting of the Hong Kong Baptist Association. With the chairman's support, the Association members voted to constitute a College Preparation Committee. This was the third general strategy. The fourth and final strategy involved the matter of representation on the Committee. Again it was deemed necessary to obtain interested influential Chinese and Missionary representatives on the Committee.

The Chinese members of the Preparation Committee included the Association Chairman and other Chinese influentials. Included was an architect, who had also been successful in business. [3]   Other important members were pastors, school administrators and teachers and businessmen. A young newcomer to Hong Kong, who strongly influenced the Association Chairman to appoint a College Preparation Committee was elected to its membership. [4]   He had recently come to Hong Kong with his Hong Kong-born wife from university and seminary study in the United States. His family had been prominent in

Baptist university administration in China. He had chosen to take a position in the Hong Kong Pui Ching Middle School rather than return to China, where his mother and family members still resided. He ordinarily would have returned there, had the change in the government of China not taken place. The influence of this man is seen in that he worked behind the scenes in helping the chairman make contacts with missionaries, Christian leaders, and others who could help launch the College.

The western members were selected from among about fifteen members of the Hong Kong-Macau Baptist Mission. The six persons chosen had previously held positions of prominence in Baptist organizations in China, and at the time held such positions in Hong Kong. The most influential of these missionaries was the chairman of the mission and treasurer. [5]   He also served as President of the Baptist Seminary in Hong Kong. Another missionary was the Director of the Hong Kong Baptist Press. [6]

A committee of the most influential Chinese and western Baptists was thus properly constituted in 1955, as a culmination of the first several strategies. [7]

STRATEGIES TO OBTAIN A FAVORABLE RESPONSE FROM POTENTIAL FINANCIAL SOURCES

The Association-related middle school, Pui Ching, was considered by the planners for the College to be the logical place for beginning operation. The first of the second set of strategies was then to see that several of the members of the College Preparation Committee were on the Staff or Board of Trustees of this lareg well-established Baptist high school. As it turned out, the chairman of Hong Kong Baptist Association saw to it that every single active member of the Middle School Board of Trustees was appointed to the Committee. This strategy provided for favorable Middle School trustee action, when needed.

Chinese Association members were not willing to undertake projects requiring large continuing support which did not have the financial backing of the Hong Kong-Macau Baptist Mission. The selection of several "key" missionaries to serve on the Association Preparation Committee, therefore, was an important additional strategy designed to get the missionary organization, and the parent-body in the United States, permanently linked to the college undertaking. One of the first maneuvers was to approach the members of the Mission by official letter to ask for financial assistance and for personnel to help launch and to continue to help operate the college.

The mission members, in view of the magnitude of the task, made the request for financial and personnel assistance a matter for careful discussion and consideration. They deliberated on questions such as: would the parent-body in the United States favor Mission cooperation in such an undertaking? How much of an annual subsidy would the parent-body provide? How much money would be required to provide an adequate college campus? To what extent would the college project affect adversely provision of funds for building of churches, a hospital which several were interested in establishing, and the securing of funds for an adequate seminary campus? How would missionary personnel be secured to help found the college? Who were possible prospects to help administer and teach in the college?

The Mission members appointed a committee of representatives to talk with Association leaders, especially church pastors, about the kind of college-organization needed. [8] They were to bring back recommendations. The pastors, to a man, were favorable to the establishment of a college but with certain conditions. Their support was contingent on Mission backing and the maintenance of a Christian atmosphere and program in the school.

The missionaries eventually approved of the college. However, they wanted to be sure that the school would achieve Christian goals. As a strategy to this end, they required that: (1) one-third of the trustees of the proposed college should be missionaries, (2) all other trustees would be chosen by Association members or possibly a few by similar bodies from some other Asian countries [9] and (3) the Association should be responsible for an initial donation of not less than H.K.$30,000.00 for the first session. [10]

They also stated a condition that the administrative staff at the college should all be active Baptist church members, and at least sixty per cent of the teachers and staff-members should be Baptists, and all of them Christians. They further stipulated that a missionary with administrative ability should be appointed vice president of the school and should be in Hong Kong to assist in the preparations for the college opening. They proposed that the Pui Ching Middle School facilities should be used only on a very temporary basis. [11]

In responding to requests from Chinese members of the College Preparation Committee the Mission members agreed to ask the parent-body in the United States to contribute U.S.$25,000.00 for the first year of college operation, and at least U.S.$20,000.00 as an annual subsidy thereafter. [12]

A joint gathering of all the missionaries and all interested associational leaders in the Spring of 1956, proved to be a decisive meeting. The Secretary for the Orient of the Southern Baptist Foreign Mission Board paid a special visit to this assembly and spoke formally to the group. [13] The missionaries had been so divided on the issue of founding the college that the Secretary for the Orient's address was later edited by him and circulated. [14] In general, the gathering was told that the Association must take full responsibility for operating the college and must assume increasing financial and administrative responsibilities. The Southern Baptist Foreign Mission Board would agree only on these conditions to supply limited funds for operation and capital needs. Immediately after the circulation of the above letter, the Hong Kong Baptist Association approved the financial plans for the college. This assurance was enough for the members of the College Preparation Committee to decide to launch the college in September, 1956. The strategy to get American mission board backing although precarious was successful. The second set of the college had succeeded.

STRATEGIES FOR THE CREATION OF AN ADMINISTRATIVE STRUCTURE

Once decisions relative to the organization and financing of the college were made, it became necessary to think of an administrative structure. The College Preparation Committee, had completed its charge of making a recommendation to the Association and was formerly dissolved. The Association then proceeded to appoint a Board of Trustees. It was logical that most of the members of the former Preparation Committee appear on this Board. This was the first of the strategies followed to create an administrative structure. Nine missionaries, nine members of the Middle Schools' Board, and nine persons from the community were chosen to serve on a Board of Trustees. [15]

The second of these strategies to develop an administrative structure highlights the delicate nature of East-West relations.

At the first formal Board meeting, the trustees elected officers and appointed a small committee to nominate a President and a Vice President.

The trustees informally agreed that the President should be Chinese. Christian universities established in China toward the end of the nineteenth century, or the beginning of the twentieth, had opened with westerners as chief administrators, but by the 1930's and 1940's Chinese leaders were firmly committed to elect Chinese as heads of their major organizations. For example, the Chung Chi College, the first Christian college established in the Colony had a Chinese president. It was true, the University of Hong Kong had a British administrator. However, this was considered appropriate for an English-language, Government-operated university in a British Colony. Actually, the Governor of Hong Kong was the Chancellor (a more-or-less honorary position, although he presided at important convocations when degrees were conferred).

There was never a real question as to the choice for President. The Chairman of the Association, who was also Principal of Pui Ching Middle School, was the logical prospect. Although he spoke of his own incompetence to administer a university and the heavy responsibilities he already shouldered, it was evident he would accept the post. When he was not made Chairman of the Board of Trustees it was a clue to the strategy that he would be chosen for the Presidency.[17] The strategy unfolded in this manner.

It was pointed out that the President of Hong Kong Baptist College would represent the college in conferences with Government officials and take major responsibility for fund-raising, securing a site, and negotiating at the highest levels on behalf of the college. Then, it was stated that the associational chairman was acquainted with leaders in Government, business, education, and religion, having grown up in the Colony. It was also brought out that his contacts, especially in the Christian circles, were broad, extending to the United States and England. Also, it was known that he would serve without salary, an important consideration for a school with meager support. Once these points were made his nomination and election proved a foregone conclusion.

It was a condition of the missionaries that the Vice President of the college should be a westerner and a member of the Hong Kong-Macau Baptist Mission. This had been a necessary strategy both to maintain western support and to achieve smooth university operations. The fact that important administrative assistance could be obtained without the need for renumeration was also an important consideration. The pattern of electing a western Vice President had been followed in the establishment of the Chung Chi College in Hong Kong.

The Trustees elected the writer who was serving as Director of the Baptist

Press to be Vice President. The members of the Hong Kong-Macau Baptist Mission, upon receipt of a formal request, approved his serving as Vice President. They stipulated, however, that he must, continue to serve with the Baptist Press until a missionary replacement could be appointed. [18]

The President and Vice President immediately assumed these offices. The Vice President, at the request of the President, also served as Dean of Studies. The strategy to set up an administrative structure including a Chinese President and a western Vice President had been accomplished.

STRATEGIES TO SECURE GOVERNMENT APPROVAL TO OPERATE

The Baptist leaders planning for the Hong Kong college were quite sure that another post-secondary college would meet a need and get enthusiastic response from the community. The only Chinese-language Christian college in the Colony was an interdenominational school named Chung Chi. This college had a strong student appeal. Of the other colleges in Hong Kong, New Asia, affiliated with Yale University, was at that time oriented toward Taiwan and emphasized Chinese literature, history, and philosophy, rather than science or business. The newly-formed United College was still suffering from internal conflicts and had no auspicious foreign connections. It, too, did not offer the popular science courses. Chu Hai, and several other less-known colleges, had Taiwan connections, but seemed to get less-qualified students, since the universities of Taiwan accepted the most promising secondary school graduates from Hong Kong.

The need for a college was also related to another fact. In the early 1950's graduates of middle schools interested in science and engineering, especially, were still going to Mainland China universities for schooling. However, by 1955 the general political climate in Hong Kong was against study in Mainland China.

The timing to found a new college seemed to be strategic as far as the economic situation was concerned. By 1955 the economy of Hong Kong was beginning to accelerate, and there were many indications of steady growth and improvement. The Government Department of Education and private operators were opening more primary and secondary schools which needed teachers. Welfare agencies were in need of social workers. The building industries were thriving and calling for workers. Church-related agencies were looking for college-trained personnel. With all of these factors in mind, the planners for Hong Kong Baptist College were confident that a ready-employment market was available for its graduates. In this regard, it was evident that the Government-supported university and colleges were not supplying enough graduates to meet local needs.

The reputation of the Baptist-operated schools, Pui Ching and Pooi To, was good. For this reason it was felt that a close relationship with the Pui Ching school would be especially useful to a new Baptist college in getting Government approval, as well as for the other reasons. The Baptists of Hong Kong had achieved considerable success in fostering secondary education. They had worked quite harmoniously with educational authorities in this connection.

The Hong Kong Education officials responded favorably and without delay to the application for the establishment of a Baptist college. Furthermore, informal assurance was given that a site for a permanent campus would be available. However, there was no promise of further financial assistance or recognition.

The Baptist leaders wanted a "Chinese-language" college for purposes of sentiment and self-esteem. They also wanted an emphasis on the teaching of Chinese literature, history, philosophy, and other cultural subjects, which they felt would help preserve the good, as conceived by Christians, in traditional Chinese culture. Both of these ideas were acceptable to British Government authorities. If the plan had been to establish an English-language post-secondary school it would likely have been blocked, since the English-language University of Hong Kong was considered adequate to meet needs for such university training. However, Hong Kong Chinese students, who formerly could study in Mainland China universities, in addition to "refugee-students" from China were in need of good educational opportunities. Furthermore, the British Government policy of little or no interference with the customs and practices of Chinese in Hong Kong was favorable to traditional cultural subjects. Thus, the first strategy to obtain political approval was successful.

Government registration required both a Chinese name and an English name for the school. Chinese Baptists also considered a suitable name vital for their own legitimization and support of the school. Considerable discussion ensured among Board of Trustee members as to an appropriate name. The missionaries had suggested that it be called Southeast Asia Baptist University. Most of them were anxious to keep "Baptist" in the name. There was some talk among the Chinese of calling it Pui Ching (Baptist) University, as a strategy of getting support of the active and prosperous alumni associations (in several parts of the world) of this school. However, the Pui Ching Trustees, who were also on the College Board, were not ready to push the idea. At the first meeting of its members in March, 1956 the Board of Trustees selected the English name, "Hong Kong Baptist College." The equivalent in Chinese, " 浸會學院 ," was informally agreed upon after several hours of discussions, since these were various Chinese characters to express the same idea. The problem was the stipulation of the Government Department of Education that the characters " 浸會書院 ," and not " 浸會學院 " should be used to designate such a college. The characters " 大學 " which signify a university, and the characters " 學院 " which signify a college of a university, could not be used. [19]

The last of the strategies for obtaining approval to operate was a Constitution. All official documents in Hong Kong must be in English. Consequently, the Trustees had to require and approve a bi-lingual Constitution.

The Constitution required much thought and revision before its final adoption, but represented the culmination of the strategy to gain Government recognition. [20]

STRATEGIES TO OBTAIN FAVORABLE PUBLIC ACCEPTANCE AND COMMUNITY SUPPORT

The Trustees of the college knew that the college had to be conceived of as both necessary and legitimate by the Hong Kong community. Since it was newly established, and since its founders intended to perpetuate both denominational and general norms, special strategies in public relations were in order.

The first public relation strategy was the projection of an image of quality education, adequately financed, and characterized by East-West cooperation. To this end, it was seen that both Chinese and English-language newspapers announced the foundation of the proposed new college. The articles emphasized the American base of support and the possible affiliations with Baptist universities in the United States. Also, the prospectus of the college, (See

E.D. 2
1,000-9/59-B11672

Ref. No. E.D. 1/28174/56

FORM 2
表格二

|s. 10(3)|

EDUCATION ORDINANCE, 1952
一九五二年教育條例

Certificate of registration of School
學校註冊証書

This is to certify that the under mentioned school has been registered under the Education
茲　查　下　述　學　校　業　遵　照　一　九　五　二　年　教　育　條　例　之　規　定　愛　配　合　行　登　給
Ordinance, 1952.
學校註冊証書此証

Registered name of school
學　校　註　冊　名　稱
(in English) .... **Hong Kong Baptist College**
(英文)

Registered name of school
學　校　註　冊　名　稱   香港浸信會書院
(in Chinese)
(中文)

Type of school—day/evening .... **Day School**
何　種　學　校　——　日　校/夜　校

Address: 80, Waterloo Road, Kowloon.
校　址

(C. T. KELL)
p. *Director of Education.*
香港教育司

Hong Kong, 11th December, 19 63.
一千九 年 月 日

N.B.: This school was originally registered
on 20.12.1956 under the same name at the same
address.

WARNING
警　告

Registration of a school does not release the management committee or the proprietors
學　校　之　註　冊　並　不　能　帶　免　該　校　校　董　或　校　主　等　遵　守　一　九　五　五　年　建　築
from compliance with any relevant requirements of the Building Ordinance, 1955, or any other
條　例　或　其　他　條　例　之　責　任　亦　並　不　因　該　校　則　已　註　冊　而　致　影　響　或　更　改　一　搬　有
Ordinance, nor does it in any way affect or modify any agreements or covenants whatsoever relating
關　設　置　該　物　作　爲　學　校　用　途　之　合　約
to the premises intended for use as the school.

ILLUSTRATION 1
Certificate of Registration, Hong Kong Baptist College

Illustration 2, pp. 57-58), prepared in English and Chinese, was circulated widely at schools and other centers. These notices together with Chinese newspaper advertisements publicized the college among Middle School graduates and their families. Special action was taken to be sure that a large number of students from the Baptist-related Pui Ching and Pooi To Middle Schools would apply for the entrance examinations. The registration in large numbers from these very acceptable middle schools was important to impress students and teachers in other organizations that the college would be of high academic quality.

The Baptist church leaders, as well, in their Sunday announcements and bulletins gave out information about the opening of the college.

The President had a large circle of governmental, church, business and other acquaintances and friends in the Colony. He was constantly in attendance at dinner parties and other functions. Not infrequently he attended three such occasions in one evening. His attendance called attention to the new college, and when called upon to speak, he never failed to mention the new Baptist College.

The western Vice President and the Chinese Dean of Students both became members of the Kowloon Rotary Club in 1956. No other college or university was represented in service clubs. In this way many leading Chinese and European business and professional people came to know and accept the Hong Kong Baptist College as a respectable institution of higher learning. The Dean of Students also worked closely with the alumni associations of the thirteen Christian Universities of China, which had large memberships and active programs in Hong Kong. He arranged for the college administrators to get acquainted with some of these leaders. In the above ways a favorable public image was developed in the Hong Kong community.

It was necessary to get good publicity abroad as well as at home. Just prior to the opening of the school, the president-elect was at Oklahoma Baptist University for the conferring of an Honorary Doctorate, and took the opportunity to tell about the college.

Releases were given Baptist World Alliance and Southern Baptist Convention editors of newspapers and magazines about the plans to open the Hong

1. PURPOSE: The purpose of the College is to provide a Christian environment in which young people may study and be trained on the Post-Secondary School level and to give them specialized training plus a general knowledge of both Western and Chinese cultures, in order that they may serve well both God and man.

2. LOCATION: For the time being Pui Ching Middle School, Waterloo Road, Kowloon, Hong Kong has kindly made available classrooms and office space. We are now looking for a permanent site.

3. DEPARTMENTS:
   Chinese Literature and History   Religion and Philosophy
   Foreign Languages and Literature   Business Administration
   Sociology and Education   Mathematics and Science
      Civil Engineering

4. APPLICANTS ACCEPTED: Freshman students will be accepted for the Fall Semester in all Departments.

5. QUALIFICATIONS FOR APPLICATION TO TAKE ENTRANCE EXAMINATIONS: Graduates of Senior Middle Schools, who have official diplomas or other certificates signifying that they have finished Senior Middle School, and/or Hong Kong students who have passed the Government School Leaving Examinations, are eligible.

6. REGISTRATION FOR ENTRANCE EXAMINATIONS:
   Place: The Office of the Baptist College in Pui Ching Middle School, 80 Waterloo Road, Kowloon, Hong Kong.
   Date: From the present to July the 7th.
   Procedure: Students who come to register for the Entrance Examinations must bring their diplomas and school grades and six photos and pay HK$10.00 Examination fee. Each applicant will complete forms and get an identification number for the Entrance Examinations.

7. ENTRANCE EXAMINATIONS:
   Location: Pui Ching Middle School, Senior Department, Waterloo Road, Kowloon, Hong Kong.
   Date: July 9th (Monday), 9:00 A.M.

8. SUBJECTS: All students will take examinations in Chinese, English, and Mathematics.

9. SCHOOL TUITION: HK$300 for a Semester (Payment may be made monthly at HK$50.00 for five-months).

10. MATRICULATION AND THE BEGINNING OF CLASSES:
    Matriculation: September 10, Monday
    Formal Opening of School: September 11, Tuesday, 10.00 A.M.
    Beginning of Classes: September 12, Wednesday

11. SCHOLARSHIPS:
    (1) Five students who make the highest grades in the Entrance Examinations will be awarded full scholarships or half scholarships for the first semester.
    (2) If the five seniors with the highest averages from a recognized high school upon the recommendation of their principal all take entrance examinations the two students in this particular group making the highest averages will be granted full scholarships for the first semester.
    (3) The College will offer scholarships to students who have real financial need. Any student with a good scholastic record can apply for a scholarship. After investigation by the scholarship committee he will be granted a full or partial scholarship, as long as such funds are available.
    (4) All of the following may apply for a half scholarship for their children or for themselves.
       (i) Pastors and full-time ministers of Protestant Churches.
       (ii) Full-time staff-members of Baptist Institutions.
       (iii) Students who have dedicated their lives to full-time Christian service.

1956-1957 PROSPECTUS

Hong Kong Baptist College

一九五六—一九五七年

香港浸會書院章程

院 長 林子豐博士

副院長 晏務理博士

ILLUSTRATION 2

Hong Kong Baptist College prospectus, 1956-57

Lam Chi-Fung, LL.D. President
Maurice J. Anderson, Th. D. Vice President

附註：
申請退讓助學金須填具表格，經院務會議通過，始於入學之後...

C. 凡在校肄業學生經教職員會議議決於本院工作之學生工作人員。
B. 本院教職員兼任各科形之教師及工讀身兼本院工作之學生工作人員。
A. 凡本院之職員及其家屬身兼本院工作之學生工作人員。

（四）有本學院成績優良之學生得領本院所設之名額獎助學金。
（三）凡本學院成績優良而經濟困難之學生得免本院所訂名額助學金。
（二）凡入本學院前一學年成績優良者得領本院所訂名額獎學金。
（一）凡...入本學院者...得領本院所訂名額獎學金。

十一、獎助學金

十、註冊日期
（一）正課上課日期：九月十日（星期...）
（二）...：九月十日（星期...）
（三）...：九月十日（星期...）

九、學費
每一學年學費港幣...元，每月分一次繳付，或分次數繳付一次繳清等三種。

八、考試科目
國文（星期...）打字...考試...成績...以九年中學...

七、考期
手續：由本院於九月...發表取錄新生...榜...七月正取生...備取生...中學以上學校

六、報名

五、招生
公立及私立...及...本院招收一年級新生

四、工商管理系、土木工程系、...

三、...系院：
文史系、外國語文系、經濟系、數理系、體育系...

二、...

一、宗旨：本學院...以培養...人才...以溝通中西文化，發揚中國文化...

ILLUSTRATION 2 (Continued)

Kong college. The interest in the college by overseas, especially American persons, was fostered by the pervious missionary work in China. The world Baptist community was thus seen as providing a large potential following.

STRATEGIES TO BEGIN THE OPERATION OF THE COLLEGE

It will be recalled that the Pui Ching Middle School campus was to be utilized by the new college. The Trustees of the college were careful to follow protocol in official relations between the Chinese President of the college who was at the same time Principal of the Middle School. Often the latter found himself corresponding as President of Hong Kong Baptist College with himself in his position as Principal of Pui Ching Middle School. Persons in both organizations prepared these letters for his signature. Often it was strategic for the western Vice President to make approaches to the Vice-principals (two of them) of the Middle School. He went out of his way to pay the proper respect in relations with these Vice-principals.

Perhaps the most basic need in the operation of a college is a faculty and staff. The President's recommendations were that two staff members; the Dean of Students, and the Librarian who would also serve as teacher of English, be elected first. [21] The Dean of Students was to serve without salary, since he was already on the staff and received his salary from the Middle School. The Librarian and Teacher of English was to be engaged at a salary of H.K.$1,200.00 per month. These two persons were expected to assist with all the necessary details for opening the college in September. These persons were by temperament and ability capable of working with both the Chinese and western administrations and to facilitate the business and academic preparations necessary. This was itself a part of the strategy of operation.

Major responsibilities in preparing for the first session of the school thus fell on the Vice President and Dean of Studies, the Dean of Students and the Librarian and Professor of English. These three officers worked in unison to prepare for the opening of the school in September. Division of labor worked itself out without formal authorization.

After space and a core staff were provided, the next strategy for becoming operational was to employ a capable staff and faculty. All of the staff were recruited from Baptist church members. They were either new college and university graduates or were transferred from the Baptist Press.

The task of securing teachers was completed by the opening of school. Persons with higher degrees in their fields, or with previous university and/or research experience, were selected as a policy matter. Other things being equal, Chinese Protestant Christians and persons who could teach either in Cantonese, Mandarin or English were engaged. Preference was given active members of the Baptist church. Teachers were not selected if they were known to be Communist sympathizers or militant Nationalists. Only three full-time appointments were given. Part-time lecturers as needed, were engaged to complete course offerings. The starting full-time salary for a Ph.D. was H.K.$1,200.00 per month on a twelve-month basis. Moderate monthly increments would be given for each additional year of service. Persons with Master's degrees would start at H.K.$1,050.00 per month, and persons with Bachelor's degrees, plus university teaching experience, would start at H.K.$900.00 per month. Special consideration would be given to experienced professors without these qualifications. Part-time teachers were paid at the monthly rate of H.K.$80.00 for three teaching hours per week. This scale was in line with salaries in other post-secondary college.

Summarizing, there were three full-time lecturers, nine Chinese teachers on part-time salaries, and eleven western teachers, who served without salary. They were all secured prior to the opening of the session. This made a total of three full-time and twenty part-time teachers for the first year. [22]

The next need was for equipment. Funds from the Mission were available for furniture, equipment, and books. [23] The Dean of Students was responsible for the purchase of necessary supplies and equipment. He made decisions as to the use of facilities available to the college in the Middle School. [24] The Librarian, however, personally ordered and supervised the building of library furniture. She made purchases of initial books and periodicals on her own authority. Both worked effectively when allowed this freedom of action, and such effective work was necessary in view of the shortness of time before the opening of school. The newly equipped offices, classrooms, and library were in readiness when students first came in July for entrance examinations.

The organization of departments of study was next in strategy procedures. It was known that departments and courses must have the approval of the

HONG KONG BAPTIST COLLEGE

Courses	Present Enrollment		Total Enrollment
	Male	Female	
Business Administration	12	3	15
Sociology	4	20	24
Foreign Language and Literature	20	14	34
Mathematics and Science	20	7	27
Civil Engineering	41	2	43
			143

Course	Section		Professor	Number of Students	Sex		Room Number
					M	F	
English	01	(1)	Grace Chen	35	25	10	B, C
English	101	(2)	Grace Chen	36	26	10	B, C
English	101	(3)	C.W. Leung	37	30	7	A, B, C
English	101	(4)	Grace Chen	39	24	15	A, B, C
Chinese	101	(1)	N.Z. Zia	35	25	11	A, C
Chinese	101	(2)	James Mau	36	26	10	A, E306
Chinese	101	(3)	N.Z. Zia	37	30	7	A, B
Chinese	101	(4)	N.Z. Zia	39	24	15	B, C
Chinese	101	(1)	C.Y. Hsu	36	25	11	A, C
History							
History	101	(2)	C.Y. Hsu	36	26	10	B, C
History	101	(3)	C.S. Wong	37	30	7	C, E101, E310
History	101	(4)	C.S. Wong	39	24	15	A, C
Sociology	101		M.J. Anderson	38	6	32	B
Mathematics	101	(A)	E. Yang Yu	40	36	4	A
Mathematics	101	(B)	E. Yang Yu	43	29	14	A
Mathematics	121		E. Yang Yu	41	34	7	A
Physics	101	(1)	E. Yang Yu	42	39	3	C
Physics	101	(2)	E. Yang Yu	43	39	4	B
Geology	101		C.F. Wong	43	42	1	B
Economics	101	(1)	S.K. Hoh	16	10	6	A
Economics	101	(2)	Y.P. Chau	17	7	10	B
Accounting	101		I.L. Cho	32	13	19	A
Biology	101	(1)	K.W. Yum	37	16	21	A, B
Biology	101	(2)	K.W. Yum	20	13	7	A, B
Bible	101	(1)	J.D. Belote	25	23	2	A
Bible	101	(2)	V. Frank	25	24	1	B
Bible	101	(3)	C. Morgan	14	8	6	C
Bible	101	(4)	M.J. Anderson	27	19	8	Re. P.
Bible	101	(5)	J. Hollis	26	17	9	B
Bible	101	(6)	Mrs. S. Rankin	26	5	21	C
English	101	(1)	Mrs. J. Belote	27	19	8	Re. Cp.
Conversation							
Conversation	101	(2)	Mrs. C. Morgan	26	17	9	P. Lab.
Conversation	101	(3)	Mrs. M.J. Anderson	26	5	21	Re. P.
Conversation	101	(4)	Miss Inez Chow	25	23	2	B
Conversation	101	(5)	Mrs. S. Rankin	25	24	1	Re. P.
Conversation	101	(6)	Miss B. Groves	14	8	6	C

ILLUSTRATION 3

INFORMATION SHEET PREPARED IN 1956 TO SHOW COURSES, TEACHERS, NUMBER OF STUDENTS, AND LOCATION OF CLASSES

Director of Education for the Hong Kong Colony. It was also felt necessary that a Christian college have a Department of Religion. In like manner, a Chinese college must have a Department of Chinese. Sociology, Foreign Languages and Literature, Business Administration, Mathematics and Science and Civil Engineering Departments were also part of the initial plans.

The Director of Education in Hong Kong approved all of the departments and courses. However, few or no students applied for the Department of Religion or the Department of Chinese. This, in view of the strategic importance of both departments to the existence of the college, was an interesting development. Fortunately, all of the students were required to study Religion and Chinese as first year orientation courses, and arrangements already made for faculty did not have to be altered.

The last part of the strategy to begin operations related to admission requirements. Three major subjects were included in the examination given, Chinese, English and Mathematics. The examination was developed by the faculty members employed. Faculty and staff were present in force to assist with the administration of the first entrance examination, attended by over 200 candidates. System and order and good planning were in evidence. The examinations were conducted in an efficient business-like way to impress the prospects for admission to the first class. Adequate luncheon arrangement for candidates were made at the Middle School cafeteria. Of those who passed, over 100 registered for entrance to the college. In August more than 100 students sat for a second examination. In view of this number college faculty and administration were confident of a successful opening.

ANALYSES AND CONCLUSIONS

System Characteristics of the Embryo Organization

The embryo Hong Kong Baptist College system can be analyzed in terms of the characteristics of open systems as identified previously.

Importation of Energy. The communication and interaction which ensued since the first individual discussed his ideas with another can be seen as energy inputs into the Hong Kong Baptist College system. Information served to link in a common task such sub-groups as the Pui Ching Middle School Trustees, the Hong Kong-Macau Baptist Mission members, and their American-based headquarter elites; and the Government of Hong Kong through the officials in its Education Department with the members of the sponsoring association. Material vehicles in the form of space, facilities, money, and regulations were other forms of input; as were the personnel provided for the system. All of these sources of input were inparted from the outside, since system had the only an emergent structure.

Cycle of events. The embryo system, through the institutionalization of a constitution and other operational procedures began cycles of events which will be repeated annually. This will be true even though there is a reordering of the units or a further differentiation of functions. Cycles can be seen in the less regular intervals of meetings of the Board and in the activity necessary to process materials, personnel and students.

Negative entropy. The growth of the Hong Kong Baptist College is dependent on the ability its actor-members will have to make it prosper. Steps such as securing a suitable name for cultural legitimization, and a constitution to comply with Government requests and bring order to the system were designed to secure the system's continued viability. Energy expended to get a permanent site, and to maintain open communication-links among the various actors are in the interest of negative entropy. Positive entropy will be in evidence if and when the college begins to deteriorate noticeably.

Negative feedback. The units in the embryo system, which continued to increase and to be differentiated as the system developed were those parts which had outside environmental contacts. These contacts gave clues (feedback) as to when the system might be off course for survival. Negative feedback, for example, was a factor which caused the Trustees not to use "Pui Ching" or leave out "Baptist" in the name. It resulted in officers employing personnel to eliminate certain individuals from consideration for the faculty and staff. It affected the tuition-charge and scholarship arrangements which were finally announced.

Differentiation. From the very beginning the system differentiated between the functions of its component parts. The election of officers and appointment of committees started the differentiation. As the system continued to be structured, further differentiation in functions of administrators, Chinese and western, developed. The President began to devote his energies to community contacts, while the Vice President concentrated on the preparations within the projected system for input and throughput. As the Vice President and the other officers operated in the system each specialized in his area of competence. This process of preparation for the throughput continued as each specialized unit was added and fitted into the same system but with more and more minute division of labor.

ANALYSIS OF BEHAVIORAL STRESS IN THE EMBRYO ORGANIZATION

The behavioral model used for analyzing the stress and strain as a normal organizational feature, was described earlier. Here the stresses related to survival strategies of the emergent college organization are pinpointed in some detail.

It will be shown how combinations of diverse cultural expectations made for maladjustments and latent, if not manifest, strains. Although the missionaries involved had lived and worked in China, and in Hong Kong, their basic socialization was quite alien to that of their Chinese counterparts. However, they together with the Chinese actors described were accustomed to playing roles in a variety of group settings. The situation was not as bad as though individuals of diverse cultural backgrounds were suddenly thrown together. Yet, reciprocal expectations between Chinese and western actors were different in most instances from expectations of Chinese toward Chinese or westerners toward westerners.

1. *Role conflict.* Role conflict, as pointed out previously, occurs when two of an individual's roles are not compatible. In the effort to establish Hong Kong Baptist College role conflict was more obvious among Board of Trustee members than elsewhere. Stress arose in that some of the missionary trustees found themselves playing roles in helping to develop a system which they thought should not exist and about the functioning of which they had negative feelings. In the Mission and in private they had opposed the founding of the college. They had gone along with the decision to open the school with 'tongue in cheek,' and by election to a controlling unit of the system found themselves playing roles due to felt obligations and perceived pressures.

2. *Role incongruity.* Incongruity in roles occur when rewards and other positive sanctions are out of balance with the demands of a role. The Chinese President and western Vice President, although apparent logical choices for the roles they were to play in the system, were placed in situations of potential incongruity. The President's station was by far the highest in the college. He was expected to be a prestige-giver, fund-raiser, and chief agent for replenishment of energy from the outside environment. However, the location of his office outside the college complex and delegation of many of a resident's

functions to either a western Vice President, the Chairman of the Board, or the Dean of Students, left him almost entirely out of the interaction by which he could have been identified as the most functionally important unit in the system. In other words he did not receive all the prestige and honor of his position.

The Vice President, by contrast, was often expected to function as the academic officer in the system. In fact he appeared to many to be the functional head of the college. Yet, he did not receive the rewards of such a position.

3. *Role inadequacy.* Role inadequacy results when an actor is forced to play a role for which he is not prepared or qualified. In the emergent Hong Kong Baptist College situation, the President often asserted, and many thought it was true, that in spite of his station in the community he was inadequate for the role he played in the system. He, as a successful and influential semi-retired business man, may have served the system better as chairman of the Board. He professed to know little about college education in general and management of a college system in particular. He did not have a university degree, nor was he conversant with authority relationships which were expected to prevail between expressive elites, like professors in the school and the administrative officers of a college. His experience in business and Middle School management was more related to controlling instrumental officials who were more liable to accept his style of management. For these reasons it was fortunate that he committed the employment of professors and relations with them to his western counterparts. Nonetheless, his sense of role inadequacy in the initiation of the organization likely was more responsible for his lack of participation in the important formative processes, than his desire to delegate these functions to others.

The western Vice President was put in a position in which he could not exercise the normally expected role behavior toward the Chinese President. There were language barriers, although each could speak in some fashion the language of the other. In technical conversation neither understood the other well enough to get fine meanings across, and the use of interpreters never made for meaningful direct communication. Beyond this barrier was also the differences in educational backgrounds, expectations as to the functions of college officers, and conceptions of what a college should be like. These differences were not due so much to diverse Chinese and American backgrounds, but rather to other cultural factors. There were polite gestures due to different cultural backgrounds which had to be played out during time which may otherwise have been spent in meaningful consultation. Others had varying degrees of role inadequacy. Many of the faculty, for example, were not accustomed to a church related school environment.

4. *Role non-reciprocity.* Role non-reciprocity is in evidence when one actor fails to react to another. This situation occured in the formative period of Hong Kong Baptist College in this manner. The western Vice President, because of the absence of the President developed a close working relationship with the western-educated Chinese Chairman of the Board. Many times these two, had to chart the course of Board meetings and in many respects the development of the whole college organization. Often, however, these plans were not approved, and Board meeting time was wasted due to this non-reciprocity. The President, not having been a part of the planning, and sensing a threat to his position refused to interact. This action blocked business which was recognized as useful to the system. The President usually sought to demonstrate his functional importance by reiterating familiar information about his plans or wishes for procurement of funds, government contacts and the like. The group-members, impatient with his time-consuming act, used a tactic of suggesting that the meeting end.

5. *Role frustration.* When an actor knows how to play a role, but does not have the necessary facilities, he experiences role frustration. All of the members of the college were required to perform some roles for which they had inadequate facilities. The most obvious need was for money for needed equipment, books, *et cetera*. The young Dean of Students was especially frustrated because what he had in Hong Kong did not compare to what it would have been in his native Shanghai, where his father had been the President of the Baptist-operated university. He was given the title of "Dean of Students," which was satisfactory in itself, but which brought frustration when he was expected to function in a way which anticipated the normal accoutrements of such an office, including performance tests, advisors, records and the like.

It can be seen from the above that tension and stress were probably present to a greater degree than normal for such an emergent organization. Also, these stresses were unique in some ways because of the cultural factors involved.

---

1. Records of incorporation are kept by the officials in the Headquarters Building, Kowloon, Hong Kong. It will here after be referred to as the Hong Kong Baptist Association.
2. He was Dr. Lam Chi Fung.
3. He was Dr. David Y.K. Wong.
4. He was Mr. Franklin K.S. Liu.

5. He was Dr. James D. Belote, the present Secretary for East Asia of the Southern Baptist Foreign Mission Board.

6. The writer of this report.

7. Hong Kong Baptist Association Annual Meeting Minutes (in Chinese) 1955.

8. Hong Kong-Macau Baptist Mission Minutes (March and June, 1955), p. 13. These records are on file at the Mission office, 169 Boundary Street, Kowloon, Hong Kong, and the Foreign Mission Board, Southern Baptist Convention headquarters, Richmond, Virginia.

9. *Ibid.*, pp. 16-18.

10. One U.S. dollar at that time was equivalent to H.K.$5.70.

11. Hong Kong-Macau Mission Minutes (September and December, 1955), pp. 5-6, 26-27.

12. *Ibid.*, pp. 21-23.

13. He was Dr. Winston Crawley, now Overseas Secretary for the Southern Baptist Foreign Mission Board.

14. A copy of this address is on file at the Hong Kong-Macau Mission office.

15. Hong Kong United Christian Baptist Churches Association Minutes in Chinese (1956) located at Association Headquarters, Waterloo Road, Kowloon, Hong Kong.

16. Hong Kong Baptist College Board of Trustee Meeting Minutes, March 6, 1956.

17. Dr. David Y.K. Wong, referred to in the previous section, was chosen for this position.

18. The writer of this report became the missionary Vice President of the college.

19. See Illustration 1, p. 55, for a copy of the Certificate of Registration on which the correct Chinese name of the school is written in both English and Chinese. In many publications and on some letterheads the more impressive Chinese characters 學院 , are used. The college leaders considered it inappropriate to use the same characters to designate the post-secondary colleges as was used to designate secondary schools, and less prestigious schools which could not confer degrees.

20. See Appendix A for the English version of the original Constitution.

21. Franklin Liu, son of the former president of Shanghai University, studied at Baylor University, Waco, Texas, and Southwestern Baptist Theological Seminary, Fort Worth, Texas, where he earned Master's degrees in Business Administration and Religious Education, respectively, before returning to Hong Kong in 1953. He met and married a Hong Kong girl while at Baylor. At the change of governments in China in 1949, his mother and brothers and sisters were in Shanghai. His father several years before, had been assassinated during the Japanese occupation of Shanghai. He accepted a position as Religious Director in the Pui Ching Middle School, and never was reunited with members of his own family in Shanghai, although he had occasional telephone conversations and letters from them. He was primarily interested in serving in a college, and was mentioned in the previous section as one of the first promoters of the college plan. He was considered to be the president's right hand man. A lady, Dr. Grace Chang, had completed her Doctorate in the United States and had been on the staff of the Carver School of Missions and Social Work (now incorporated into the Baptist Seminary) in Louisville, Kentucky. She had been in Hong Kong for a short time and was an editor in the Baptist Press, but the salary there was very low and it was the consensus of missionary friends and Chinese that she was most suited to transfer to the more responsible and better-paying college position.

22. See Illustration 3, p. 61, for a copy of an information sheet prepared in 1956 which gives the names of all the teachers.

23. Hong Kong-Macau Baptist Mission Minutes, June, 1956, show that U.S.$5,000.00 became available for furniture and equipment, and U.S.$10,000.00 was granted for library books.

24. Use of these facilities was provided upon a formal request by the college in February, 1956. See Board of Trustee meeting minutes for March 5, 1956.

CHAPTER VII

STRATEGIES OF ORGANIZATIONAL OPERATION: THE FIRST FOUR YEARS

INTRODUCTION

The description and analysis in this chapter pinpoint the strategic actions employed during a four year period necessary to process the first class of students at Hong Kong Baptist College. These actions had to do with the provision of necessary space, as well as facilities and funds. Also, strategies related to problems of faculty and staff, general school policy, student recruitment, and training and public relations had to be worked out during this period.

The college assumed the characteristics of a modern open system, including many behavioral stresses. In the discussion which follows this fact will become clear as will the continuing processes of a morphogenic nature which characterized this new and growing organization.

The information, unless footnoted was obtained by the writer, who was a participant observer for three years of the period covered in this chapter. The remaining year he was in close touch with the college authorities, especially the missionary who acted in his place.

STRATEGIES DESIGNED TO PROVIDE THE NECESSARY SPACE, FACILITIES, AND FUNDS

Obviously, space, facilities, and funds are foremost considerations for a new venture, such as a college. Therefore it is apropos to review the strategies employed relative to the fulfilling of these needs for the first four years of college operation. The goal was to service the student population at something like a satisfactory level.

The first strategy was to maintain good relations with Pui Ching Middle School. This was necessary to retain exclusive use of a building for college headquarters, classrooms and other facilities. The usual procedure was for the Trustees of the Hong Kong Baptist College to send letters of thanks to the middle school Trustees (many of whom were also on the College Board), each year. [1]   Criticism, however, had come at the beginning of the third year, when the college authorities enclosed a terrace on the second floor of the headquarters' building without permission. This necessitated strategic action including apologies as well as thanks. [2]   The college authorities requested the use of facilities for the 1959-60 session almost a year in advance as a consequence. [3]

The strategies related to facilities involved several other deliberate moves designed to minimize behavioral (structural) stresses. The latter were inherent in the close and frustrating working conditions which were necessary. Some of the mechanisms used to prevent stress situations from arising were as follows:
(1)   During class breaks the noise from high school students was so great that college students often could not hear what lecturers were saying. Furthermore, classes were disturbed by loud talk or curious students passing by or lingering outside to hear what was being said. College authorities did not wish to antagonize middle school staff or students by complaining, and made the best of the situation.
(2)   Strong efforts were made to obtain additional funds and usable equipment from private sources as well as college support sources. The first years obviously found the college with many needs and few resources. It was thus that a planned campaign to inform the public generally of needs was instigated. However, the strategy of this campaign was subtle. On the one hand the appearance had to be given that the college was a going and strong institution. On the other hand the many needs for books, laboratory equipment, office equipment, *et cetera*, made it necessary to solicit help. The strategies of this nature involved among other things deliberate attempts to get funds from visitors from the United States. In this connection each year western guests were shown the college and entertained at dinner by the President. Missionaries and Chinese teachers were present to talk with them. Gifts were presented on most occasions.

All westerners apparently went away with a good impression of the faculty and a warm feeling for what was being done for needy students.

Although the various moves to obtain funds and usable items from private sources enjoyed only limited success at first, there were later benefits.

The records show that the strategy of entertaining western guests to add to operating funds began to pay off in money and goodwill after a time. The total expenditures from 1956-60 for supplies, equipment, and books are shown in Table II. Operating funds were more difficult to obtain and necessitated other strategies. For one thing, as many missionaries, and other volunteer

TABLE II

EXPENDITURES FOR SUPPLIES, EQUIPMENT, AND BOOKS
HONG KONG BAPTIST COLLEGE, 1956-60

Item	Cost
General Furniture and Office Equipment	H.K.$ 73,280.43
Library Furniture and Equipment	16,175.30
Library Books	76,286.54
Laboratory Equipment	160,663.35
TOTAL	H.K.$326,405.62

Source: Statements of Accounts, Hong Kong Baptist College, 1956-60, Lowe, Bigham, and Matthews, chartered accountants.

workers as could be recruited were used. Others were employed on a part-time basis. In this way the limited funds were stretched and the appearance of a large faculty given. In this regard all funds available were used with great frugality and care. There was no possibility of raising tuition during this period since students were financially impoverished.

STRATEGIES TO WORK OUT PROBLEMS RELATED TO
STAFF AND FACULTY AND TO ESTABLISH
PERMANENT ADMINISTRATIVE POLICIES

The administrators of Hong Kong Baptist College were aware that the success of the venture depended to a great extent on the quality of the staff and teachers in the college and the administrative policies. The aim was to maintain a teaching and extra-curricular program second to none of the other post-secondary colleges in the Colony.

The foremost consideration had to be economy of operation. It has already been mentioned that one strategy was to employ Baptist Chinese refugees and young college graduates and to ask for voluntary missionary help.

As more students enrolled, more staff were needed. However, applications to the Mission Board for help were not successful until the beginning of the fourth session, when three missionaries were made available for staff duties.

Economy as stated was an important consideration in getting a faculty. Besides asking for missionaries one strategy was to get local persons who were known to be good teachers part-time. Some of these teachers had studied abroad but on returning to Hong Kong assisted in family business undertakings. Others were teachers in the post-secondary colleges and needed to "moonlight" to add to their low incomes. A few were Baptists with teaching obligations elsewhere but interested in helping the new school.

Another strategy was to get exchange teachers from Baptist colleges and universities abroad who were available without pay. The Foreign Mission Board provided funds for their travel and the college provided for their living accomodations.

Still another strategy was to arrange with the American Consular officials for American exchange professors to teach part-time at the college as well as in the university and the Government subsidized post-secondary colleges. This kind of help brought prestige to the Hong Kong Baptist College.

During the first session only three full-time teachers, were employed. They all were Chinese and Christians. Twenty part-time teachers were employed. Many were missionaries who had seminary training as well as university degrees. They were suitable primarily for the Bible and English conversation courses. Six full-time teachers were employed for the second session, along with a full-time exchange teacher. There were thirty part-time teachers for this term, eleven missionaries and nineteen Chinese. There were nine full-time teachers for the third session. There were only five volunteer missionary teachers among the twenty-seven who taught on a part-time basis. The nine full-time teachers mentioned above continued to teach for the fourth session. Six more were added to make a total of fifteen for the term. In addition there were twenty-eight part-time teachers, only five of whom were missionaries.

It can be seen considerable success in strategies to develop a faculty was achieved. Fifteen full-time persons had been enlisted by the fourth year of operation. The goal to maintain a predominantely Christian faculty was achieved. Exchange relations had developed with two Baptist-related schools in the United States. The help of the American Consulate in getting exchange professors succeeded for the last two sessions.

One of the full-time teachers had the Ph.D. degree from an American university. Four teachers held M.A. degrees from American universities, and one had taken his degree in China. Two had Seminary training beyond their B.A. degrees. Seven had Bachelor degrees. All had teaching experience in their fields. Twelve of them were men, and three were women. Thirteen were Chinese, one was British, and another Filipino.

After teachers, the college was in need of energetic administrators. The strategy of the Board of Trustees had been to appoint, along with the President, two administrators approved by him who were thought capable of developing an educational system. These persons were chosen so as to gain the acceptance of a variety of groups. The organization began operation in 1956, therefore, with three persons in administrative roles.

The President was in communication with Trustees and devoted time and energy setting the stage for fund-raising and public relations. Many Chinese and western guests visited with him. He daily signed the college checks. Administrative authority in daily operation was exercised mainly by the Vice President assisted, when needed, by the Dean of Students. However, there was little direct communication among the three administrators. Recognized cultural differences made polite gestures and courtesies a necessity when they were together, but this did not facilitate the operation of the school. The President never presided over faculty and staff meetings and had little contact with faculty and staff members. The meetings were conducted in English and presided over by the Vice President. The faculty and staff understood the Dean of Student's special relationship with the President and sought, therefore, not to antagonize either of them.

Loose-coordination and independence of action characterized the administration in policy matters during the four year period. This made for a comparatively smooth operation, but set the stage for the appearance of stress as the interaction and communication among the administrators became more frequent, as the next chapter will show.

STRATEGIES DESIGNED TO WORK OUT PROBLEMS IN STUDENT RECRUITMENT, DISCIPLINE AND TRAINING

The purpose for which the organization was established, was the teaching and training of students. The processes of recruitment in these formative years and the quality and quantity of students trained were important for the immediate period as well as the future. The teaching and training offered during these four years would determine the quality of graduates produced and be reflected in feedback from the external environment. It is, therefore, appropriate to trace the strategies employed in the recruitment and processing of students.

Student recruitment. The quality of students who applied for admission to the Hong Kong Baptist College was varied. The college entrance examinations in Chinese, English, and Mathematics were designed to eliminate poorly prepared candidates and to select the better qualified students. The strategy was to enroll all who passed the examinations and a few others whose application for admission were supported by influential persons, so as to operate the school at full capacity and to gain public support.

In 1956, 192 candidates took entrance examinations and 153 matriculated, although several of them never enrolled in classes.

The enrollment by departments in October, 1956 was as shown in Table III on the opposite page.

TABLE III

HONG KONG BAPTIST COLLEGE
ENROLLMENT BY DEPARTMENTS IN OCTOBER, 1956

Department	Number of Men	Number of Women	Total
Business Administration	12	3	15
Sociology and Social Work	6	21	27
Foreign Languages	15	14	29
Mathematics and Science	20	6	26
Civil Engineering	37	2	39
TOTALS	90	46	136

Source: Faculty and Staff meeting Minutes, October, 1956.

Thirteen different courses were offered as shown in Table IV.

TABLE IV

HONG KONG BAPTIST COLLEGE
COURSES OF STUDY AND STUDENT ATTENDANCE
1956-57

Name of course	Lecture hours per week	Number of sections	Total number of hours	Number of students
Chinese	3	4	12	37
Chinese History	3	4	12	37
English	3	4	12	37
English Conversation	1	6	6	24
Bible	2	6	12	24
Accounting	3	1	3	32
Biology	3	2	6	27
Economics	3	2	6	16
Geology	3	1	3	43
Mathematics, regular	3	2	6	52
Mathematics, advanced	3	1	3	41
Physics	3	2	6	43
Sociology	3	1	3	38
TOTAL	36	36	90	38(Mean)

Source: A statistical report (see Illustration 1, p. 50) from Registrar's office records, 1956-57.

In 1957 the number of applicants for admission to the college increased to 270, and 214 enrolled. [5]   The proportion of Pui Ching and Pooi To students in this class was less than in the previous year. [6]

The enrollment for 1957-58 is given in Table V, below.

TABLE V

HONG KONG BAPTIST COLLEGE
ENROLLMENT SUMMARY, 1957-58

1957-58 Session	1st Year			2nd Year			Grand Total
	Men	Women	Total	Men	Women	Total	
Foreign Languages and Literature	38	7	45	5	3	8	53
Sociology	14	27	41	8	17	25	66
Business Administration	26	16	42	11	3	14	56
Mathematics and Science	32	13	45	11	8	19	64
Civil Engineering	38	3	41	36	1	37	78
TOTAL	148	66	214	71	32	103	317

Source: Hong Kong Baptist College Catalogue, 1957-58, p. 48.

It can be seen that the number of students enrolled in each of the five departments at the beginning of the 1957-58 session was about equal in number.

In 1958, 468 candidates took examinations for first year admission. A total of 284 were matriculated.

The enrollment for 1958-59 is given in Table VI, on the opposite page.

TABLE VI

HONG KONG BAPTIST COLLEGE
ENROLLMENT SUMMARY
1958-59 SESSION

Departments	1st Year			2nd Year			3rd Year			Grand Total
	Men	Women	Total	Men	Women	Total	Men	Women	Total	
Foreign Languages and Literature	21	21	42	17	10	27	3	- -	3	72
Sociology	14	36	50	22	27	49	7	16	23	122
Business Administration	31	14	45	21	15	36	12	1	13	94
Mathematics and Science	62	26	88	22	9	31	7	5	12	131
Civil Engineering	54	3	57	47	- -	47	33	1	34	138
TOTAL	182	100	282	129	61	190	62	23	85	557

Source: The Hong Kong Baptist College Bulletin, 1959-60, p. 62.

The enrollment for 1959-60 is shown in Table VII, below. During that

TABLE VII

HONG KONG BAPTIST COLLEGE
ENROLLMENT SUMMARY
1959-60 SESSION

Departments	1st Year			2nd Year			3rd Year			4th Year			Grand Total
	Men	Women	Total	Men	Women	Total	Men	Women	Total	Men	Women	Total	
Foreign Languages and Literature	15	21	36	11	7	18	13	2	15	3	1	4	73
Sociology	7	36	43	18	21	39	9	21	30	5	12	17	129
Business Administration	26	16	42	28	12	40	17	10	27	8	2	10	119
Mathematics and Science	37	21	58	40	21	61	9	6	15	6	4	10	144
Civil Engineering	45	1	46	47	1	48	31	1	32	31	1	32	158
TOTAL	130	95	225	144	62	206	79	40	119	53	20	73	623

Source: The Hong Kong Baptist College Bulletin, 1960-61, p. 53.

session first year enrollment was more evenly distributed among the departments than in the previous years, Mathematics and Science had the largest number of students.

Data about 606 students, almost all those enrolled for 1960, gives a picture of the educational and geographical background of the student body recruited. First, second, and third year students were grouped together in the summary and Seniors were tabulated separately. Also, schools attended were classified as Chinese or English.

Among sixty-five Seniors, forty-six students, or 87 percent, were from Hong Kong and Mainland China; six students, or 9 percent, from Macau; and three students, or slightly over 4 percent, from Taiwan and Indonesia. Among the remaining 541 students, 467, or 86 percent, were from Hong Kong and Mainland China; forty-three students, or 8 percent, from Macau; and thirty-one students, or 6 percent, from eight other Southeast Asian areas. Among the Seniors, fifty-eight persons, or 88 percent, were from Chinese-language Middle Schools, and eight persons, or 12 percent, were from English-language Middle Schools. Among 541 students in the first three years of study 479 persons, or 87 percent, were from Chinese-language schools. Only sixty-two persons, or 13 percent were from English-language schools. [7]

Requests came every year to admit students who failed the entrance examinations or did not take them. They came from Board members, pastors leading citizens, Government officials, and from the faculty and staff of schools and colleges. If examination records were exceptionally poor, such requests were rejected. Some "recommended students" with better records were admitted "on probation" or as "special students".

Special problems were faced in the admission of pre-theological students. If such students were recommended by seminary officials, they were admitted regardless of entrance examination results. The number, though small, added to the problem of maintaining a uniform entrance standard by the school. Students from Mainland China posed another problem. They could get no official records. They could only produce Chinese school admission cards. Their foundations in English and Chinese Literature and History were often weak, but their preparation in Mathematics and the Sciences was usually excellent. It was considered expedient to admit such students, even if they failed English and Chinese examinations. Students, all Chinese, from other areas of Southeast Asia posed problems as well. Tentative admission must be given months in advance to make possible the issuing of visas to study in Hong Kong. Occasionally, they arrived in Hong Kong on visitors' visa or by illegal means. Some were than admitted out of compassion.

The strategy to admit all who measured up to the educational requirements, and others as pressure, diplomacy, and compassion dictated resulted in wide representation among Chinese-language schools especially and from schools in several countries of Southeast Asia. Two or three times as many students applied as the college accepted.

Scholarships. A strategy to get superior students from the start was to admit those who made highest grades on college entrance examinations free of charge. Foreign Mission Board subsidy designated for scholarships, could be used to help needy students. Success in recruiting and enrolling students was partially due to the generous scholarship policy they made possible. Tuition assistance given during the first session was as follows:

Type	Number
Half tuition Scholarships	60
Full tuition Scholarships	5
Full work Scholarships	7
TOTAL	72[8]

In 1957 seventy-three of the 103 students who returned to the second year class, received tuition assistance. One hundred and three of the 214 in the new first year class received tuition assistance. A number of denominational groups and other bodies such as the College Student Work Project committee also provided help to students. [9] During the third session, 1958-59, 298 students out of a total of 516, were assisted. A majority of students for the 1959-60 session also received scholarship assistance. [10]

Student Discipline and Training

Orientation. Many students had never attended a Christian school. The first days of orientation, thus, acquainted them with the program of the college. The strategy was to convince them that the Baptist College had a superior program academically and otherwise. The officers told about American university connections and the possibility of transfer to American colleges, and the desire of college faculty to help those who graduated with good records to pursue further studies in the United States. The Christian backing and support of the school was stressed. At the same time it was made clear that all students were admitted and treated equally and without reference to religious affiliations or interests.

Student activities. In many countries students are active in promoting their own social activities. Patterns of dating, and related social events set the stage for most activities. In Hong Kong, however, most of the post-secondary students were not accustomed to dating. At parties and dinners men and women tended to avoid each other. The strategy was to encourage development of social as well as cultural and professional interests and to develop loyalty to the college. Beginning with the first session a Student Day program became an annual event. During the second session departmental societies were organized. A faculty sponsor for each society was named. However, society activities depended almost entirely on student initiative and leadership. Holidays and weekends provided the only desirable meeting times. Picnics and outings were occasionally planned on those days with or without the help of sponsors. [11]

A strategy to develop student loyalty was cleverly promoted in the first year. Contests to provide the school seal and chorus was fostered (see Illustration 4 and 5, pp. 82-83). In the second year students were enlisted in selling raffle tickets to raise money for the college. During the third and fourth sessions over seventy-five students joined the newly formed Dramatics Club. Activities centered around ticket-selling and the presentation of a play to raise money for the college. [12] The student yearbook, published for the first time in 1960, provides the best record of student activities during that period. [13]

Student assemblies. Students from Christian middle schools were accustomed to religious services. However, many Hong Kong Baptist College students had never attended such meetings, nor had they ever been to church. Consequently, the authorities took special measures to ensure order and cooperation at assemblies.

The strategy was to warn students that cooperation was mandatory. Outstanding Chinese ministers and musicians who could hold the interest of students were brought to the school. Visitors from overseas and missionaries were often asked to speak. The novelty of hearing a westerner, and the advantages of listening to English, made for better attention. When important visitors, especially westerners were present, all were better behaved. Those who misbehaved were

ILLUSTRATION 4

The Hong Kong Baptist College Seal

校　歌
COLLEGE ANTHEM

ILLUSTRATION 5
The School Chours of the Hong Kong Baptist College

later scolded by the Dean of Students.

Religious activities. The Hong Kong Baptist College officers were committed to promote Christian activities on campus. The strategy was to provide an
adequate staff to supervise activities, and funds were provided to subsidize the
program.

A Religious Director was employed beginning with the 1957-58 session.
He taught Bible classes and so was too busy to promote student activities.
During the 1959-60 session a missionary and a Chinese youth worker came from
the United States as advisers. They developed an organization patterned after
the American Southern Baptist Student Union. Only one religious organization
was permitted on campus, and it was college policy that its officers be Baptists.

Religious Emphasis Weeks. A purpose of the school was to give students an
understanding of and an opportunity to embrace Christianity. However, few local ministers were invited to assist in this goal. A strategy of getting western
ministers to lead Religious Emphasis Week services was followed.

Table VIII, below gives the dates, names and positions of persons who

TABLE VIII

RELIGIOUS EMPHASIS WEEK SPEAKERS AND DATES, 1956-60

Date	Name	Position	Nationality
1956 October	Dr. Forrest Feezer	Executive-Secretary, Texas Baptist Convention	American
1957 November	Dr. Roland Brown	Evangelist and Former Baptist Pastor, Chicago, Illinois	American
1958 March 24-28	Dr. Edwin B. Dozier	Missionary to Japan	American
1958 October 22-24	Rev. Paul Smith	Minister, Tabernacle Church, Toronto, Canada	Canadian
1959 March	Dr. David Morken	Evangelist, with Headquarters in Hong Kong	American
1959 November 7-11	Dr. Lewis Salter	Physics Professor on the Kentucky team in an Indonesian univer-sity	American
1960 March 22-25	Dr. Leon Chow	Taiwan Baptist Theology Professor	Chinese

Source: Records in the Director of Religious Activities' office, 1956-60.

were engaged to speak from 1956 through this four year period. Only one Chinese was engaged for these meetings. He was from Taiwan and had been trained in the United States.

Table IX shows the religious affiliations of the 1960 graduates both at the

TABLE IX

HONG KONG BAPTIST COLLEGE

RELIGIOUS AFFILIATIONS OF GRADUATES, 1960

NAME OF DEPARTMENT	TOTAL NUMBER	RELIGION ON ENTERING THE COLLEGE				RELIGION AT GRADUATION			
		Baptist	Other Protestant	Catholic	None	Baptist	Other Protestant	Catholic	None
Foreign Languages	4	0	2	0	2	0	2	0	2
Sociology	18	5	4	0	9	7	6	0	5
Business Administration	6	0	1	1	4	1	2	0	3
Mathematics and Science	9	2	2	0	5	4	4	0	1
Civil Engineering	29	2	2	0	25	8	3	0	18
TOTAL	66	9	11	1	45	20	17	0	29

Source: Records of the Registrar and the Director of Religious Activities, 1956-60.

time they entered the college and at the time of their graduation. A significant number became Christians during their four years in college.

Classroom instruction. Hong Kong Baptist College students attended classes taught both by westerners and Chinese, and the language of instruction was either Cantonese, Mandarin, or English. Most texts and reference materials were in English. A strategy to assure effective learning was the requirement that students must have some knowledge of Chinese and English before entering the college. When texts were used in introductory courses, regular courses took a year to complete.

Teachers followed the lecture method, and little time was given to discussion. Lectures in "broken" English by Chinese professors were often difficult to understand. Furthermore, teachers who spoke in Cantonese or Mandarin often had pronunciations colored by the dialects of their native villages. Chinese professors often spent classroom time translating course texts.

Westerners most often used English as the medium of instruction. The language had to be simplified, and the use of blackboards and mimeographed notes was frequent. Teachers tended to follow the textbooks, since outside assignments added to the confusion. A few missionaries lectured in Chinese. Their tonal errors provided occasions for amusement and jokes.

Crowded homes made study difficult. Many students went to libraries and study centers to find comparative quiet. A short supply of textbooks was a common problem. The school bookstore stocked old editions of standard texts at small cost but teachers, often insisted that up-to-date editions be used. Students then sought "pirated" editions of texts printed in Taiwan and illegally sold in Hong Kong.

Examinations were taken seriously. Failure on examinations meant "losing face," but the enrollment policy and high academic standards made failure a foregone conclusion for many.

Student defection. It is normal for colleges to have dropouts. Since most colleges have considerable income from sources other than tuition and are in a position to collect student fees a semester in advance, budgets are not seriously affected by such dropouts. However, the Hong Kong Government stipulated that student tuition be paid in ten equal instalments. This helped to foster instability in student enrollment. A school dependent on tuition income could be ruined financially by a heavy dropout. The strategy of the school authorities was to admit a large number of students, with the expectation that many would dropout. For this reason, class sections were overloaded at the beginning of the session.

Student's reasons for leaving school were not accurately determined. Knowledgeable persons suggested that those better qualified in English and the more affluent students left to go abroad for study. Some dropped out for financial reasons; others because of poor grades. By tracing the class of 1956 year by year until graduation in 1960 one can see how department enrollment was affected through the four year cycle. Table X on page 88 shows this process.

The graduates. Sixty-six students completed the four year cycle and were graduated in July, 1960. One of them was chosen from among outstanding Hong Kong College and University students to represent the Colony on a special tour of the United States sponsored by the American Consulate. [14] A western-type Baccalaureate service and Commencement Ceremony were held for the graduates. [15]

The faculty discovered that the averages of nine students were slightly below the necessary standard. They then agreed that a quality point average near 1.0, i.e., 0.90 or better, would be treated as standard. One student who had not completed two required courses, but had more than enough credits, was allowed to graduate. [16] Two students who failed semester courses took and passed make-up examinations. One student, partially blind, passed all courses, but his quality point average was below 0.9. By producing doctor's evidence of partial blindness, he received permission to graduate as an exceptional case. [17]

The faculty, held opposing viewpoints, with regards to graduation standards. The strategic actions taken in 1960 to resolve this stress set the stage for repeat performances during the years to follow.

Table XI on page 89 shows the range of grades (in terms of quality points) by department for the 1960 graduating class.

The faculty and staff assisted in the placement of graduates in positions in the community and in graduate schools overseas. Graduates were permitted to apply for a special course for post-secondary college graduates in a Hong Kong teacher training college. [18] More than half of them applied. [19] Many also applied for graduate study abroad and positions in the Colony as well. [20]

By November, 1960, graduates were engaged as shown in Table XII on page 89.

TABLE X

HONG KONG BAPTIST COLLEGE

DROPOUT OF STUDENTS IN THE THROUGH-PUT: ENTERING CLASS, 1956-1960

Departments	1st Year			2nd Year			3rd Year			4th Year		
	Male	Female	Total	Male	Female	Total	Male	Female	Total	Male	Female	Total
Business Administration	12	3	15	11	3	14	12	1	13	5	1	6
Sociology	6	1	7	17	8	25	7	16	23	13	5	18
Foreign Languages	15	14	29	3	5	8	3	0	3	1	3	4
Mathematics and Science	20	6	26	11	8	19	7	5	12	1	8	9
Civil Engineering	37	2	39	36	1	37	33	1	34	28	1	29
TOTAL	90	46	136	71	32	103	62	23	85	46	20	66

Source: Records in the Registrar's office, 1960.

TABLE XI

QUALITY POINT AVERAGES OF GRADUATES, 1960, BY DEPARTMENTS

Department	Male	Number Female	Total	Number with Distinction*	Range	Average
Foreign Languages	2	2	4	0	1.0-1.6	1.2
Sociology	6	12	18	2	1.0-2.2	1.5
Business Administration	5	1	6	2	1.1-2.2	1.7
Mathematics and Science	5	4	9	3	1.0-2.4	1.6
Civil Engineering	28	1	29	5	0.9-2.5	1.4
TOTAL	46	20	66	12	0.9-2.5	1.5

*Distinction was given to students with quality point average of 2.0 or more.
Source: Records in the Registrar's office, 1960.

TABLE XII

LOCATION OF HONG KONG BAPTIST COLLEGE GRADUATES IN NOVEMBER, 1960, TWO MONTHS AFTER GRADUATION

Location	Number
Graduate Study in the United States	12
Hong Kong Architect and Engineering Firms	15
Accounting and Commercial Firms	6 6
Social Welfare Agencies	7
Middle School teachers	5
Baptist College or other Baptist organization's staff	7
Teachers Training College	5
Awaiting employment	8
TOTAL	66

Source: A Report of the President to the Trustees, November 17, 1960.

Feedback came from firms, agencies and schools where graduates served or continued to study. The major criticism was that the graduates' ability in English was not adequate. They were highly praised, however, for hard work, a sense of responsibility and faithful service.

STRATEGIES IN PUBLIC RELATIONS PROBLEMS

Alignments. Obviously, to legitimize and develop a university the founders intended to find additional resources in the local community and overseas. However, alignments with the American Southern Baptist Mission Board and the Hong Kong Baptist Association imposed serious limitations. Baptist control must be maintained even if other denominations, the Hong Kong Government, and private bodies gave support. The American Mission Board officials, and the local Hong Kong-Macau Baptist missionaries together with most local Baptists, agreed on this point. It was clear the college could not compete with church-related projects to get funds. The strategy therefore was for fund-raising efforts to be carried out in the United States and that these efforts be directed by Chinese (not missionary) personnel. Also, such solicitations had to be restricted to non-publicized methods acceptable to Mission Board officials in the United States.

The first strategy was thus to maintain a strong, stable alignment with the Foreign Mission Board (and the Hong Kong-Macau Mission). The Hong Kong-Macau Baptist Mission organization was the important link between the Association officers and the American Mission Board, whose officers were responsible to make decisions affecting the college. An acceptable procedure for communication between the Mission officials and the Association officials had to be followed. Since the college was sponsored by the Hong Kong Baptist Association, its Trustees were expected to address requests for operating funds and missionary personnel as well as for building and other capital needs, by official letter to officers of the Association. Such letters were passed on to the Mission. Replies to requests had to follow precisely the same procedure in reverse order.

Chinese leaders often looked upon the above indirect communication method as time-consuming and unnecessary red-tape. Often they did not take it seriously. The Vice President, consequently, had to see to it that the protocol was followed as much as possible.

Another strategy was to inaugurate action at the administrative level (without reference to the Trustees) to secure Government recognition and material resources. When and if Government officials responded favorably, the Trustees would be called upon to act in the light of the situation prevailing at the time.

The Hong Kong Government announcement in April, 1959 that three competitor colleges would receive large annual operating grants alerted Hong Kong Baptist College officials to the difficult position they faced. In 1957 informal approaches had been made to Hong Kong Baptist College to affiliate with a Joint Council of the three above-mentioned colleges, but the matter had not been presented to the Trustees for consideration. Joint Council members were not able to admit the Baptist College now that Government subsidy and control was in sight. A high-level Government decision to assist only the three new member colleges had been made and no other school could participate in the plan. (See Illustration 6, p. 92, for the Government's explanation to the public).

Obviously something had to be done to obtain Government support. The strategy employed by the Hong Kong Baptist College Trustees was to amend the constitution, so as to be eligible to register as a post-secondary college under the new Government ordinance. Hong Kong Baptist College officials intended to press for this registration.[21] There was hope of admission into the new university system being established. A law firm was engaged to facilitate incorporation of the college as a step toward registration. The new constitution was adopted and a new method of electing Trustees followed.[22] Fortunately, missionaries and middle school Board members heartily approved of the change, and so no strain developed because of it.

Support. The first strategy to get community support was for members of the college staff to join organizations of potential support. The Chinese and western administrators attended meetings whenever possible to represent the college. They accepted responsibilities on committees and in other ways. The President circulated in the Chinese groups, while the Vice President circulated in bi-racial groups fostered by westerners in Hong Kong. College officials enter-tained American diplomats, and British officials stationed in the Colony, and a variety of local people. Material about the college was circulated, to the group; and the program and needs of the school discussed.

Most Hong Kong residents read one or more of the Chinese-language

Press Release.

POST-SECONDARY COLLEGES.

1. The Director of Education to-day made a further statement
   on Government's plans for the development of the post-
   secondary colleges, and the eventual establishment of a
   Chinese University.

2. Mr. Crozier said that under the provisions of the Post-
   Secondary College Bill which Government proposes to
   introduce it would be open to every post-secondary college
   which met the necessary requirements to apply for registration
   as an approved post-secondary college. This new recognition
   would not be confined to those colleges in respect of which
   he was prepared to recommend Government financial assistance.
   All colleges registered under the new Ordinance would thus
   be on an equal footing as far as official status was
   concerned.

3. It was not possible to indicate now which of the post-
   secondary colleges would ultimately form part of the
   proposed new university; that will depend on the
   standards of administration, teaching, examination, etc.,
   attained by the colleges themselves, and on the advice
   tendered to Government by a University Commission.

4. Colleges registered under a Post-Secondary Colleges
   Ordinance which could not reach the higher standards
   required of a university institution, or which did not
   aspire to them, would still have a useful function to
   perform and could be assured of a permanent place in the
   educational system of the Colony. Provided they adhered
   to satisfactory standards and offered courses of instruction
   in subjects related to the needs of Hong Kong, their
   diplomas would doubtless have considerable value.

ILLUSTRATION 6

*A public announcement about post-secondary education
by the Hong Kong Director of Education, 1959*

papers published in the Colony. The Chinese President was responsible for publicizing the Hong Kong Baptist College via the Chinese press. His secretary functioned as his press agent. Regular monthly donations to a Chinese agency paid off with frequent publication of articles about the college. Criticism of these articles however, was especially frequent. They were said to include exaggerated accounts of financial backing by the Baptists in the United States and of money secured in fund-raising efforts overseas. [23] It was said these accounts were the chief source of the opinion of many Hong Kong citizens that the Baptist College did not need Government or other Hong Kong support.

The Vice President prepared articles for two English-language newspapers, [24] and the publicity received compared favorably with that given to other colleges in the Colony. This coverage gave the general English reader the idea that Hong Kong Baptist College was in the mainstream of the higher educational effort in the Colony.

Since support overseas was especially important, university organizations in the United States had to be cultivated to provide opportunities for transfer for students form the Hong Kong Baptist College. The strategy was to utilize regularly and frequently the Foreign Mission Board and Baptist World Alliance news outlets. Correspondence with Baptist-operated universities in the United States was also carried out in the interest of publicity.

Fund-raising. A college normally receives most of its building funds from the community or area it serves. The founders of the Hong Kong Baptist College were aware, however, that a fairly large amount of support would come through the American-based Baptist Mission Board. A strategy to keep the college building found p ject high on the Baptist Association annual request list to the American-based Mission Board, and to raise additional funds in the United States and Southeast Asia, and Hong Kong was pursued.

In December, 1957, the President sent the Dean of Students to the United States to raise money. [25] He made an initial contact in the Chinese community in San Francisco which resulted in the first gift of U.S.$5,000.00. This was an encouragement to the young Chinese fund-raiser, who then travelled to Texas. However he had only one success in Texas, beyond small gifts -- an offer of U.S.$20,000.00 by a wealthy Baptist oilman, on condition that this sum be matched by a similar amount raised in Hong Kong. Fortunately, Baptist Association leaders conducted an effort in Hong Kong which netted enough to collect the American gift. [26]

In 1958 and 1959 the President's secretary went on a mission to Southeast Asia to solicit funds from business friends and acquaintances. [27] The President himself, with the Dean of Students, went to the United States in the Spring of 1960 for the same purpose. The result of these strategies pursued to raise funds are shown in Table XIII. It can be seen that, of the amount raised, 83 percent

TABLE XIII
SOURCES OF HONG KONG BAPTIST COLLEGE
BUILDING FUNDS, 1956-60

Source	Amount	Percent of Total
1. Southern Baptist Mission Board	H.K.$ 769,500.00	63
2. U.S.A. individuals	235,551.56	20
3. Southeast Asia	95,301.06	8
4. Hong Kong community	104,595.93	9
TOTAL	H.K.$1,204,948.55	100

Source: President's report to Board of Trustees, March 10, 1960.

had come from the United States, 9 percent from Hong Kong, and 8 percent from Southeast Asia.

ANALYSES AND CONCLUSIONS

The organizational strategies of Hong Kong Baptist College during its first four years of operation were described in the preceding discussions. They are treated analytically in this concluding section.

System Characteristics of the Organization

Importation of energy. The special gift of H.K.$50,000.00 which the Pui Ching school Trustees put into the college system at its inception was vital to the life of the newly founded system. Other inputs form the middle school had to do with space and facilities. These resources can be seen as the product of successful communication links between the authority units of the two systems.

The exchanges with Mission actors were largely in terms of soliciting money input to buy equipment and library books, and to renovate the space provided by the middle school. Further exchanges were designed to get missionaries as teachers. Exchanges with Education officials were about matters pertaining to departments of study, courses and their contents, books to be used, tuition fees, the number of students to be accommodated in rooms, and the like. Links with outside systems were also established to raise funds. These included all the contacts made in the United States and elsewhere.

The interaction and communication process followed for the working out of staff and faculty intensified in the late Spring each year as contractual arrangements came up for renewal. School authorities were usually engaged until the beginning of another session in the Fall in working out the details for teachers input.

Energy, in the sense of general systems theory, can be seen as imported into the Hong Kong Baptist College via each of the above mentioned ways.

Throughput. An organizational throughput process was begun with the first class. During the four year period, four sets of students were in various stages of processing. During the four year period of operation analyzed in this chapter the first set of students graduated. These graduates may be seen as the throughput of the college, or in other words, its product as a functioning organization.

Output. The first set of students graduated in early July, 1960. Measurements of their academic achievement was in terms of grades and quality point averages. Achievements in intra-mural and intercollegiate exchanges gave additional measures of quality. Changes in religious orientation which took place during the process were also to some extent a result of the throughput and a character of input.

Cycle of events. The four year period was the first complete organizational cycle of events. Another cycle was the annual election of Trustee officers and committees. The administrators developed loosely structured meetings for the direction of events in the college, such as arrangements for school and staff holidays, special convocations and events, and emergency situations, each of which could be seen as a cycle. Other cycles were the process of weekly, semester and session courses and examinations and the whole calendar of events.

Negative entropy. The interaction and communication among the Trustees and administrators was to keep energy flowing into and through the system, and to find new input in the interest of health and survival.

Every action which contributes to the growth and expansion of the college can be considered as contributing to negative entropy. In this regard, until the time the college begins to lose its viability, it cannot be characterized by positive entropy, except in certain specific areas.

Differentiation. As the college grew larger and its program and courses, staff and faculty more diverse the process of differentiation of function was evident. Most of the efforts in processing personnel was directed toward those who could perform in specific ways in the teaching process. It was considered most important for the system to find units which fitted a specific need, and to match actors with jobs in accordance with their specialties.

Steady state. The elites of the system watched with care the input and output of funds, defection of students, changes in arrangements for teachers and staff, and general college atmosphere. The authorities were especially alert to see that various programs of training were not out of balance. If many students used too much time in connection with a drama production, for example, there were communications to those responsible to change the situation. This can be equated to dynamic homeostasis or morphostasis.

Equifinality. The processing of actors varied considerably over the four year cycle. Students, however, had all been processed successfully enough to go out with the mark of the system upon them. Equifinality was evident in the departmental variations in course offerings, and in other ways individual graduates training program had varied. Although graduates had all successfully completed requirements, they represented a rather wide range of finished product.

Behavioral Stresses in the Operation of the Organization

Board of Trustees. During the first years of operation, as was the case in the tears of organizational genesis, interaction of Board of Trustees members was mainly in committee situations. Busy businessmen, pastors, and missionaries and other professionals, met evenings. Although some of their interaction was informal and relaxed during a dinner hour, formal meetings followed which led to behavioral stresses.

As pointed out in the previous chapter, most of the Trustees were not acquainted with the operational procedures for a college. It is thus not surprising that most of them exhibited symptoms of role inadequacy, at one time or other. They expecially seemed unable to cope with fund-raising problems. The Trustees' stress from not having fund-raising ability reached a peak when a site was selected and plans begun for new buildings. The Trustees' allocation of H.K.$2,500.00 to the fund-raising effort demonstrated to the President, who was committee chairman, the inability of the Trustee group to as much as understand the nature of large-scale fund raising. These actors, it appeared, had no conception of what it would cost to promote a campaign of the proportion required and the style necessary for success. Cognizant of their inability he took fund-raising into his own hands. The Trustees, then due to their own sense of inability, and their belief that the President must be responsible for fund-raising, approved without question whatever he proposed. Their previous allocation of a meagre amount had produced strain in their interaction with the President. This can be construed as an example of role non-reciprocity.

One Trustee with wealth, but little prominence, sensed the financial obligation which membership on the Board would likely entail. After a few meetings he felt this pressure so greatly that he immediately withdrew from the Board of Trustees. It can be assumed that a sense of role incongruity influenced his withdrawal. He apparently conceived that the wealthy Association leader, and new college President, would have functional importance in the system and thus be able to justify liberal contributions. However, his contributions would add to the development of the President's status-constellation, rather than his own, and he had no intention to be used in that way.

Missionary members on the Board of Trustees often conceived of themselves as incapable of active participation in meetings, since, in most instances, their ability to communicate in Chinese was far from adequate. When they spoke, what they said was either in English, which had to be interpreted or in inadequate Chinese which had to be explained. Furthermore, missionary Trustees conceived of fund-raising, as a role for which they were out of characters. They felt no obligation to assist in local fund-raising of any kind. Both types of behavior indicated role conflict.

The Administration. Several stresses due to maladjustment in relations between administrators occurred in the Hong Kong Baptist College operation, as described.

Interaction between the President and Vice President during the first years of college operation was usually initiated by the Vice President. The latter was aware of the expectations of the President that he should function in supervising much of the college's day-to-day operation and communicated as much of the detail of this kind as the President, often with other important matters in mind, was willing to hear.

Much of the Vice Presidential effort was intended to encourage and induce the President to take a more active role as President. The Vice President's functional importance in the developing college system was out of balance with his location in the structure. This situation can be seen as an example of role incongruity. The Vice President also experienced role frustration since he seemed to be expected to act with authority but was never given that right and never knew for sure that the Chinese President would support his action.

When the Vice President went on sabbatical leave, a young missionary acting Vice President came into the structure. He was expected to perform a role with little knowledge of the college situation. Also, an American University Dean, new to Hong Kong, served as Administrative Adviser. The situation provided an opportunity for the Dean of Students to initiate action through counsel to the new inexperienced men and to be responsible for day-to-day college operations. It put him in an administrative role of importance which did much to alleviate the frustration he had felt before the Vice President went on leave.

The return of the Vice President brought new stresses to the structure. The Dean of Students was no longer in a position to play the role as initiator of administrative action. However, he began to take issue with the Vice President's decisions and the Administrative Assistant (the former Acting Vice President) usually supported him. Tensions thus became evident in the system. The Vice President experienced frustration in that his leadership was not only questioned, but challenged week by week.

The President's relationships with all three of the above mentioned men had been cordial, but now he sensed a situation in which the Vice President was not supported by his Chinese Dean and a westerner whom he admired. The President thus was in role conflict, perceiving obligations to both westerners in the administrative group and not knowing what to do. These role stresses were soon relieved by the arrival of another American college teacher who served as Administrative Advisor. Meetings again assumed their former style, with lavish Chinese hospitality and respect for the western guests. The Dean of Students no longer was in a position to initiate criticism of projected plans.

Staff. The staff was new in managing college affairs, and untrained. They were therefore not able to function adequately. Some of them continued to hold jobs for which they were not prepared. The addition of trained western staff did not come about until the fourth year, when three missionaries, all women, came to the College. The Deputy Librarian was integrated into the library staff with no signals of stress. The Health Director, working alone in a specialized student service in which Chinese on the staff had no experience, interacted well with all. However, the new Adviser for Religious Activities experienced some role stress. The Chinese Religious Activities Director conceived of the western lady as a kind of high level secretarial help in the office. A conflict situation developed and continued until a Chinese lady, who understood the expectations of both oriental and westerner, was able to mediate by serving in the secretarial role.

Faculty. Faculty frustrations came mainly from situational factors. Office arrangements were inadequate. There was no room to study or relax on school premises. Members could hardly go and come at times due to student crowding in the halls. Classrooms were crowded and dusty. Often they could not make themselves heard in classes due to noises. All of these situational factors led to a high degree of role frustration. English teachers had language problems while Chinese teachers had trouble with English texts. Both had trouble understanding one another, because of cultural differences in experience and background.

Students. A considerable number of students experience stresses. Some had gotten into the school with inadequate preparation. Others were awaiting visas to go overseas. The greatest frustration came when three outside competitive college systems were subsidized by the Government. Most students could not understand why the Baptist College was not included. They still entertained hope that comparable recognition would be given the college which they attended. Also, there were problems of money, crowded quarters, inadequate study facilities, language, foreign teachers, and in general an alien cultural milieu.

It can be seen from the analysis in this section that the first four years of operation was a period of struggle for the western-type college in its eastern setting. A number of the problems were encountered because of stress brought into the structure by persons of western and eastern cultural backgrounds interacting in the processes of operation. The strategies which had to be used to achieve success and alleviate stress were consequently those one would not normally encounter in a western society.

------

1. Board of Trustee Meeting Minutes, September 8, 1958, are one example of this.
2. Board of Trustees Executive Committee Meeting Minutes, October 16, 1958.
3. *Ibid.*, November 17, 1958 and Board of Trustee Meeting Minutes, November 20, 1958.
4. From the Registrar's office, 1956.
5. Registrar's office records, 1957-58.
6. *Ibid.*
7. From the records of the Registrar's office, 1959-60.
8. Faculty and Staff Meeting Minutes, October 24, 1956.
9. The College Student Work Project committee administered aid for teaching and other work done in primary schools for poor children by approved university and college students. The committee represented different Protestant groups, and a staff was maintained to supervise the program which helped up to 400 students. The project was first undertaken to help refugees from China.
10. From the Scholarship record of the Dean of Students, on file in the Dean of Students office at the college.
11. *Ibid.*, May 17, 1958.
12. *Ibid.*, November 7, 1959, February 13, 1960, May 28, 1960.
13. All in Chinese, and prepared mainly by the Dean of Students, the yearbook, which beginning with 1960 has been published annually, does not highlight club or society activities, because they had not played an important role in student social life during the early years of the college.
14. Faculty and Staff Meeting Minutes, February 13, 1960.
15. Mr. George Carver a former Southern Baptist missionary on the staff of the Baptist-operated Shanghai University, who was, with his wife, an exchange professor for the second semester, 1959-60, gave the Baccalaureate sermon. Dr. W.R. White, President, Baylor University, was the commencement speaker. He and Mrs. White were in Hong Kong for a week, and he spoke at Baptist Middle School commencement ceremonies, and in churches, as well.
16. *Ibid.*, July 2, 1960.
17. *Ibid.*, July 2, 1960.

18. Faculty and Staff Meeting Minutes, February 13, 1960. Students who graduated from the three colleges in the Joint Council were also permitted to apply. Since teacher training was controlled and offered only by Government in its own schools, admission was highly regarded and allowed students who took special course to get teaching positions in Government-supported schools.

19. Faculty Academic Committee Meeting Minutes, March 30, 1960.

20. *Ibid.*, March 30, 1960.

21. Board of Trustees Meeting Minutes, April 8, 1960. Faculty and Staff Meeting Minutes, May 28, 1960.

22. Board of Trustees Executive Committee Meeting Minutes, June 20, 1959. Johnson, Stokes, and Masters served as legal counselors to the college authorities. (See Appendix C for the new Constitution).

23. Often people complained to the writer of these exaggerations by the college reporter.

24. They are the South China Morning Post and the Hong Kong Standard.

25. Board of Trustees Meeting Minutes, December 2, 1957.

26. From records in the office of the Hong Kong Baptist Association, 1958.

27. Board of Trustees Meeting Minutes, Apirl 13, 1958 and July 30, 1959.

CHAPTER VIII

STRATEGIES FOR SURVIVAL AS A FULL SCALE COMPETITIVE COLLEGE

In Chapter VI and VII the modern systems model served as a conceptual framework for the analyses of the behavioral strategies employed to open Hong Kong Baptist College and to operate it for the first four year cycle. This chapter follows the general outline of these chapters and is designed to pinpoint strategies developed to maintain the position of the Hong Kong Baptist College as a full scale competitive unit in the Hong Kong higher educational system. Again the modern open systems model provides the framework for conceptualizing what transpired during this on-going process, from 1960 to 1968.

STRATEGIES DESIGNED TO PROVIDE NECESSARY SPACE, FACILITIES, AND OPERATING FUNDS

Space, facilities, and operating funds continued to be major considerations for Hong Kong Baptist College, after the first class was graduated. For one thing, it was unusual for a college beginning its fifth year of operation to still be on borrowed premises. Furthermore, the student enrollment increased from 723 in September, 1960 to 1,368 in September, 1965. [1]

The strategy during this period was to make optimum use of classrooms. Even then the crowding was almost unbearable with over 1,300 students. It was thus a great relief when the four acre new campus and its seven story building were occupied in May, 1965, just a few weeks before the end of the session.

The amount of space, in addition to the grounds, was many times more than the total space available to the college in the middle school. A high wire fence was built to enclose the grounds, and grass and shrubs were planted. The building included space allocated as follows:

1. Thirty-one classrooms seating from thirty to one hundred and twenty students per room.
2. Administrative Offices for the President, Vice President, the Deans, Registrar, Comptroller, Business Manager, Accountant and others.
3. The Library, to house over 100,000 volumes, plus periodicals and journals.
4. A Science wing with a floor each for Biology, Chemistry and Physics.
5. Civil Engineering Laboratories for Material Testing, Soil and Asphalt testing, and Fluid Mechanics, plus mechanical and architectural drawing rooms.
6. Typing and Machines rooms for the Business Administration faculty.
7. A History Room, a Geography Room, Music Room, and a Language Laboratory.
8. A Lecture Theatre with a seating capacity of 164.
9. Private rooms and lounges to accommodate the Faculties of Arts, Science, and Business Administration.
10. A temporary Auditorium with a seating capacity of 600.
11. A student Center including an Open Lounge, Conference Rooms, and offices.
12. Religious Activities Rooms, including a Prayer Room and Offices for staff and religion teachers.
13. A Medical unit with proper examination and sick room facilities.
14. Physical Education facilities.
15. A Cafeteria and kitchen. [2]

The strategy was to move to the new campus just as soon as it was ready and to develop a program which would compete favorably with the colleges of the Chinese University. One effort in this connection was to increase the number of volumes in the library more rapidly than in preceding years. See Table XIV (on page 100) for library holdings year by year. The number of volumes increased rapidly during the 1967-68 session.

Another effort to compete favorably with colleges in the Chinese University was to purchase and add equipment for all laboratories and special courses. In this connection over H.K.$400,000.00 was spent during the 1967-68 session alone. [3]

TABLE XIV

HONG KONG BAPTIST COLLEGE RECORD OF
LIBRARY BOOKS AND PERIODICALS
1960-61 THROUGH 1967-68

Session	Total Number of Volumes	English Volumes	Chinese Volumes	English Periodicals	Chinese Periodicals	Total
1960-1961	9,650	5,726	3,924	73	13	86
1961-1962	11,568	7,250	4,318	76	19	95
1962-1963	13,212	8,620	4,592	93	27	120
1963-1964	14,618	9,567	5,051	104	48	152
1964-1965	15,689	10,243	5,446	113	39	152
1965-1966	16,600	10,800	5,800			
1966-1967	17,561	11,742	5,828	123	24	147
1967-1968	24,054	15,132	8,922			148

Source: Minutes of Faculty and Staff Meetings, 1960-68.

The additional income to further improve the college operation in general came mainly from increases in tuition fees. With an increase in student enrollment as early as 1965-66 in anticipation of the move to the new campus, and a still larger enrollment thereafter, income rose considerably. Public relations efforts also increased income from miscellaneous gifts which formerly went into the building fund. (See Table XV, page 107).

Although the salary scale for faculty was raised [4]   so as to compare more favorably with salaries at the Chinese University, the proportionate amount of the expenditures for faculty remuneration dropped. (See Tables XVI, XVII, and XVIII, pages 108, 109 and 110). A larger proportion went into salaries for the caretaker staff and for utilities, supplies, and maintenance of the new campus. Other income was used to pay back the money borrowed to erect and equip the building.

Considerable success was achieved in developing a program somewhat comparable to that of the colleges in the Chinese University. The great difference was in the number of students serviced. The teacher-student ratio was well over twenty to one, while in the University colleges it was less than ten to one.

STRATEGIES TO WORK OUT PROBLEMS RELATED TO STAFF AND FACULTY

In the 1960's many Baptist Christians and others sought staff positions at the college. Many were not skilled in the necessary techniques of a multi-group organization. However, in Hong Kong society friendship and family connections played an important role in employment. Usually a staff recommended by an influential person was employed, and intraining was a function of the officer in charge. By and large staff secured in this way learned to play their office roles in a satisfactory manner as long as the college was in the crowded middle school premises. The strategy on the new campus was for the President to exercise more authority especially in the employment of a new caretaker staff. However, he made choices on a friendship basis in several instances which created awkward situations.

The leftist disturbances in 1967, and resignations, retirements, illnesses, and deaths, immediately before and after, accounted for new personnel in many offices. Most of the new appointees, largely untrained and unskilled for work in

TABLE XV

HONG KONG BAPTIST COLLEGE

OPERATING INCOME OF THE COLLEGE, 1956-68

Session	Tuition and Fees Amount (HK$)	Percent	For Mission Board* Amount	Percent	Association Amount	Percent	Miscellaneous Gifts and other Income Amount	Percent	Total Amount
1956-57	$ 63,890.00	39.0	$ 45,241.36	27.6	---	0.0	$ 54,625.73	33.4	$ 163,757.09
1957-58	180,496.50	67.4	58,342.60	21.8	$ 20,000.00	7.5	8,841.93	3.3	267,681.03
1958-59	304,751.80	69.1	117,415.67	26.6	---	0.0	19,237.71	4.3	441,205.18
1959-60	350,866.00	64.9	150,364.47	27.3	21,990.00	4.7	16,987.45	3.1	540,207.92
1960-61	465,413.52	73.6	128,845.50	20.4	12,838.10	2.0	24,656.33	4.0	631,743.95
1961-62	517,880.00	70.8	136,930.00	18.7	12,190.00	1.7	64,171.95	8.8	731,071.95
1962-63	631,160.50	70.3	141,303.79	15.7	17,227.50	1.9	108,900.30	12.1	898,592.09
1963-64	666,715.00	74.6	138,262.60	15.5	24,635.20	3.0	61,978.61	6.9	891,591.41
1964-65	848,760.00	82.5	137,050.00	13.3	---	0.0	43,412.46	4.2	1,029,222.46
1965-66	1,082,215.00	82.4	136,800.00	10.4	---	0.0	93,699.14	7.2	1,312,714.14
1966-67	1,691,481.00	87.1	136,800.00	6.8	---	0.0	141,709.18	6.1	1,969,990.18
1967-68	2,035,730.00	78.6	140,300.00	5.6	15,000.00	0.6	334,780.48	15.2	2,525,808.48
TOTAL	$8,839,359.32	77.5	$1,466,655.89	12.8	$123,880.80	1.1	$982,551.27	8.6	$11,403,585.88

Source: *The audited accounts of Hong Kong Baptist College, 1956-68, on file in the office of the Vice President*

*At least H.K. $215,863.49, not shown in the table, was contributed for the purchase of furniture, laboratory equipment and supplies, library equipment and books, and miscellaneous furnishings to get the school started. Consequently, more was contributed during the first three years by the Foreign Mission Board than the figures and percentages show.

TABLE XVI

HONG KONG BAPTIST COLLEGE
EXPENDITURE SUMMARY, 1956-68

Session	Total Expenditure on Faculty		Total Expenditure on Staff		Combined Totals		Other College Expenditures		Gross College Expenditure	Gross Expenditure per Student	
	Amount	%	Amount	%	Amount	%	Amount	%		No.	Amount
HK$*											
1956-57	77,360.00	57.5	30,324.00	22.5	107,784.00	80.0	26,868.97	20.0	134,552.97	142	947.50
1957-58	157,330.00	63.2	50,602.10	20.3	207,932.10	83.2	41,218.99	16.8	249,151.09	316	788.40
1958-59	276,760.10	63.3	82,518.50	18.9	359,278.60	82.2	77,847.29	17.8	437,125.89	520	842.50
1959-60	367,334.30	65.6	125,256.00	22.3	492,590.30	87.9	67,378.85	18.1	559,969.15	594	942.90
1960-61	422,804.95	67.7	118,836.75	19.1	541,641.70	86.8	82,590.89	13.2	624,232.59	675	924.80
1961-62	531,417.50	70.5	126,538.85	16.8	657,956.35	87.3	95,791.80	12.7	753,748.15	746	1,010.40
1962-63	606,130.00	69.8	137,833.60	15.9	743,963.60	85.7	113,944.70	14.3	867,908.30	857	1,012.70
1963-64	605,467.50	65.3	151,361.50	16.3	756,829.00	81.6	170,477.11	18.4	927,306.11	887	1,045.40
1964-65	620,752.00	63.9	138,124.45	14.2	758,876.45	78.1	212,186.55	21.9	971,063.00	1015	956.70
1965-66	824,358.00	68.9	169,029.50	14.1	993,387.50	83.0	203,803.93	17.0	1,197,191.43	1245	961.60
1966-67	903,979.97	50.7	338,802.29	21.7	1,242,782.26	72.4	539,062.33	27.6	1,781,844.59	1553	1,147.30
1967-68	1,059,535.47	50.8	444,816.15	21.3	1,504,351.62	72.1	580,985.32	27.9	2,085,336.94	1755	1,188.20
Total	6,453,229.79	61.0	1,914,043.69	18.1	8,367,273.48	79.1	2,212,156.33	20.9	10,579,429.81	859	977.03

Source: Audited Accounts, 1956-68, Lowe, Bigham, and Matthews, chartered Accountants.

TABLE XVII

HONG KONG BAPTIST COLLEGE
EXPENDITURE SUMMARY, SPECIAL ITEMS, 1956-68

	Amount Available	Percentage of Total Budget	Religious Programs		Student Programs		Library and Laboratory		Public Relations		Miscellaneous	
			Amount	%	Amount	%	Amount	%	Amount	%	Amount	%
1956-57	HK$* 26,868.97	20.0			974.75	3.6	735.40	2.7	10,846.70	40.4	14,312.12	53.3
1957-58	41,218.99	16.8	2,943.20	7.1	3,644.60	8.9	2,943.20	7.2	14,350.67	34.8	17,337.32	42.1
1958-59	77,847.29	17.8	2,736.95	3.5	8,873.50	11.4	3,114.04	4.0	18,218.63	23.4	44,904.17	57.7
1959-60	67,378.85	12.1	4,733.33	7.0	6,522.55	9.7	7,562.23	11.2	21,191.05	31.5	27,369.69	40.6
1960-61	82,590.89	13.2	2,710.55	3.3	7,912.41	9.6	13,786.92	16.7	25,366.46	30.7	32,814.55	39.7
1961-62	95,791.80	12.7	2,866.20	3.0	11,279.35	11.8	14,561.16	15.2	27,038.84	28.2	40,046.25	41.8
1962-63	113,944.70	14.3	5,296.85	4.6	21,840.82	19.2	17,228.70	15.1	36,336.64	31.9	33,241.69	29.2
1963-64	170,477.11	18.4	5,120.45	3.0	21,975.23	12.9	16,812.86	9.9	44,087.73	25.9	82,480.84	48.3
1964-65	212,186.55	21.9	4,017.20	1.9	20,943.80	9.9	34,319.83	16.2	65,556.60	30.9	87,349.12	41.1
1965-66	203,803.93	17.0	5,953.75	3.0	27,691.05	10.2	23,429.67	11.5	56,010.66	27.8	90,718.80	44.5
1966-67	539,062.33	27.6	12,938.45	2.4	51,531.75	9.6	44,986.31	8.3	127,636.21	23.7	301,969.61	56.0
1967-68	580,985.32	27.9	15,705.10	2.7	60,077.55	10.3	63,586.87	10.9	74,643.40	12.9	366,972.40	63.2

Source: Audited Accounts, 1956-68, Lowe, Bigham, and Matthews, chartered accountants, on file in the office of the Vice President.

TABLE XVIII

HONG KONG BAPTIST COLLEGE

EXPENDITURE SUMMARY, SPECIAL ITEMS, PER STUDENT, 1956-68

Session	Total Annual Expense Per Student	Average Number of Students	Amount For Instructor Per Student	Amount for Staff Service Per Student	Amount For Other Library and Laboratory	Amount For Religious Act. Per Student	Amount for Other Student Act. Per Student	Amount for Public Relations	Amount for All Others
1956-57	HK$* 947.50	142	544.80	213.50	5.20	Combined for this year 6.77		76.40	100.80
1957-58	788.40	316	494.70	160.10	10.40	10.40	11.60	45.40	54.90
1958-59	842.50	520	532.20	158.70	6.00	5.20	15.00	35.00	86.40
1959-60	942.50	594	611.70	210.90	12.70	8.00	11.00	35.70	46.10
1960-61	924.80	675	626.40	176.00	20.40	4.00	11.10	37.60	48.70
1961-62	1,010.40	746	712.40	189.60	19.50	3.80	15.10	36.20	53.70
1962-63	1,112.70	857	707.30	160.80	20.10	6.20	25.50	42.40	38.90
1963-64	1,045.40	887	682.60	170.60	19.00	5.90	24.80	49.70	93.00
1964-65	956.70	1,015	611.60	136.10	33.80	4.00	20.60	64.60	86.10
1965-66	961.60	1,245	662.10	135.80	18.80	4.80	22.00	45.00	72.90
1966-67	1,147.30	1,553	582.10	183.80	28.60	8.30	33.30	82.20	194.40
1967-68	1,188.20	1,755	603.70	253.50	36.20	8.40	34.20	42.50	209.10
Average	977.00	859							

Source: Audited Accounts, 1956-68, Lowe, Bigham, and Matthews, chartered accountants, on file in the office of the Vice President.

such a complex organization, (with data processing and other electronic equipment) were in a difficult situation.

Five years after its foundation only one out of four teachers at the Hong Kong Baptist College was full-time. Few deans and department heads had yet been chosen. The strategy, which did not change during this period, was to continue to build a full-time faculty according to the pattern already established, but at a more rapid rate. The aim was to get teachers whose qualifications compared favorably with the teachers in the colleges of the Chinese University. This was accomplished in several ways. (1) Deans of Faculties and Department Heads were appointed and encouraged to take responsibility in faculty recruitment. (2) Young able faculty and talented graduates were given assistance to go abroad for further study. (3) Other qualified persons, mainly recent American graduates, were sought for faculty appointments. (4) Requests went to the Mission Board for missionaries with the goal of securing at least one highly trained and dedicated missionary teacher in every faculty. (5) Exchange personnel from universities abroad were sought and used where needed most. (6) Retired and semi-retired westerners, and young western college graduates on special programs, were employed, and organizations set up to screen and channel teachers into overseas' service were exploited to the full. (7) Part-time teaching personnel was used to complete the faculty needs and especially get specialists with community contacts. Characteristics of the faculty secured during the 1964-65 session are shown in Table XIX, page 112.

Beginning with the 1966-67 session, a rapid increase in student enrollment was accompanied by increased numbers of teaching personnel and further reorganization and faculty differentiation. (See Table XX for characteristics of the faculty that year on page 113)

Contractual arrangements with teachers were made annually and honored throughout the history of the school. [5]   Titles of teachers were changed, with the adoption of the new Constitution, and faculty was ranked as follows:

> Senior Lecturers
> Lecturers
> Assistant Lecturers
> Tutors or Demonstrators
> Assistants

TABLE XIX

CHARACTERISTICS OF HONG KONG BAPTIST COLLEGE FACULTY
1964-65

Departments and Major Teaching Fields	Full time Male	Full time Female	Full time Total	Part time Male	Part time Female	Part time Total	Total	Ph.D.	M.A.	Professional	B.A.	Diploma	Chinese	Western
Chinese	2	0	2	0	2	2	4	0	0	0	4	0	4	0
Foreign Languages	2	4	6	2	2	4	10	1	3	0	6	0	4	6
History and Geography	1	2	3	2	0	2	5	1	1	1	3	0	5	0
Business Administration	2	0	2	1	3	4	6	0	5	0	1	0	5	1
Sociology and Social Work	1	2	3	1	4	4	7	1	3	1	1	1	3	4
Biology	2	1	3	1	3	3	6	0	2	0	3	1	4	1
Chemistry	5	0	5	3	2	5	5	0	2	0	2	1	5	0
Mathematics	3	0	3	2	0	2	4	1	1	0	0	0	5	0
Physics	1	0	1	2	0	2	8	0	1	0	1	0	1	1
Civil Engineering	5	3	8	0	0	0	8	1	2	1	1	2	4	1
Other	1	1	2	2	1	7	7	0	4	0	2	1	3	3
TOTALS	25	13	38	16	7	23	61	3	30	5	10	12	45	16

Source: Dean of Studies' office Records, 1964-65.

Neither tenure arrangements nor a retirement benefit program was established. However, when several lecturers retired in 1967 a sum of money approved by the Governors and considered appropriate was presented to each. At the death

TABLE XX

CHARACTERISTICS OF THE HONG KONG BAPTIST COLLEGE FACULTY 1967-68

Departments and Major Teaching Fields	Full time			Part time			Total	Highest Degree Attained					Racial Composition	
	Male	Female	Total	Male	Female	Total		Ph.D.	M.A.	Professional	B.A.	Diploma	Chinese	Western
Chinese	4	0	4	5	0	5	9	0	3	1	5	0	9	0
Foreign Languages	5	5	10	5	1	6	16	0	7	2	4	3	11	5
History and Geography	2	1	3	2	0	2	5	0	4	1	0	0	5	0
Sociology and Social Work	3	7	10	7	3	10	20	3	11	2	1	3	13	7
Biology	3	3	6	0	0	0	6	1	2	0	3	0	4	2
Chemistry	3	3	6	0	0	0	6	2	0	1	3	0	6	0
Physics and Mathematics	9	1	10	0	0	0	10	2	3	3	2	0	10	0
Civil Engineering	5	0	5	3	0	3	8	0	4	1	1	2	8	0
Business Administration	3	1	4	4	1	5	9	0	0	1	1	7	9	0
Accounting	1	0	1	3	0	3	4	0	1	2	0	1	4	0
Secretarial Studies	0	3	3	0	3	3	6	0	2	2	2	0	1	5
Other	1	0	1	3	7	10	11	0	8	0	3	0	6	5
TOTAL	39	24	63	32	15	45	110	8	51	13	19	19	86	24

Source: Dean of Studies' office Records, 1967-68.

of a lecturer in 1968 the college paid burial expenses and made a donation as arranged by the Governors to his widow. A move then got under foot to get an approved retirement and teacher benefit program in operation as a strategy to provide more security for teachers.

STRATEGIES TO WORK OUT PROBLEMS OF STUDENT RECRUITMENT, BEHAVIOR, AND TRAINING

The process of recruitment during the 1960's was influenced by factors in the external environment including the formation of the Chinese University of Hong Kong and an increase in the number of middle school graduates. The trend was also in the direction of more students from English-language schools than Chinese-language schools. The strategy of the college in recruitment and training shows the interplay between two viewpoints. Some administrators were in favor of a large enrollment and many of the faculty were in favor of a smaller more selective student body. The fact that the administrators' viewpoint prevailed had an effect on strategies which ensued in the training process.

Recruitment and enrollment. It was customary in Hong Kong to recruit students by means of entrance examinations. By 1960 a post-secondary College's Entrance Examination Syndicate was established. This examination body became the one and only recruitment channel of the three Government subsidized colleges. Other post-secondary college officials were invited to use the examination. A small fee was charged for participation.

A first strategy was to participate in the Joint Entrance Examination but to administer a Baptist college examination as well to be sure to get enough students to meet budget requirements from student fees.

From 1960 through 1963 enrollment in the Baptist College freshman class was as follows:

Year	Number of Students
1960	258
1961	333
1962	409
1963	458 [6]

Approximately fifty each year were from the Joint Entrance Examination. Table XXI (page 115) shows the matriculation results from 1964 to 1968.

With the passing of time a larger percentage of students was recruited from the English-language middle schools. A survey in 1964 of 461 first year students

TABLE XXI
HONG KONG BAPTIST COLLEGE ENTRANCE
EXAMINATION AND MATRICULATION RECORDS
1964-68

Year	Number of Applicants	Number who passed	Number who matriculated
1964	1,021	658	505
1965	1,048	695	530
1966	1,197	856	636
1967	1,731	1,099	867
1968	2,264	1,262	1,194

Source: Registrar's Office Records, 1964-68.

showed that 66 percent were from Chinese-language schools and 34 percent from English-language schools. At the same time, among 356 upperclassmen, 69 percent were from Chinese-language schools and 31 percent from English-language schools. [7]   Thus by that time approximately one-third of the student body was from the English-language middle schools.

Another survey of 718 first year students done in 1966 showed that 431 or 60 percent, had graudated from Chinese schools, and 287, or 40 percent, were products of English schools. [8]   Thus, the percentage of students from English schools continued to rise.

The survey mentioned above also showed that 124, or 17 percent, of the students were from families whose total income per month was under H.K.$500.00. Three hundred and five, or 42 percent, were from families whose income ranged between H.K.$500.00 and H.K.$999.00 per month. One hundred eighty-five, or 26 percent, were from families whose income ranged between H.K.$1,000.00 and H.K.$1,999.00 per month. The remaining 104 students or 15 percent said the income was over H.K.$2,000 per month.

Scholarships. The college authorities continued to administer tuition grants to needy students until the Fall of 1967. Several factors led to a change that year. (1) The Foreign Mission Board had ceased sending its annual subsidy with a designation for scholarships. (2) The limited staff could not investigate family conditions of applicants as enrollment increased. (3) Students appeared to be more affluent, although many continued to apply for tuition help. (4) Money for a Loan Fund came to the college from the Mission.

Few students applied for a loan when the fund was announced, and needy applicants either sought work or were recommended for assistance elsewhere. The new strategy to substitute loans for outright grants was successful and demonstrated that the college no longer needed tuition grants to attract as many students as it wished to enroll.

Discipline and Training

Orientation. There was little change in the orientation process, except that efforts to impress entering students were no longer made. The number of entering students became so large that the strategy was to divide them into several groups for better communication during orientation sessions. They were also required to attend a formal convocation held in a large church building some distance away, so as to bring them all together.

Much of the formal orientation on the new campus was correlated with the programs of the student societies. Since every student was enrolled in one department or another, most of the social life centered around these society organizations. By getting acquainted with the officers and meeting some of the older students at welcome parties, a new student began to feel that he belonged to the new college organization. After the student association began to function in 1967 the officers participated in the orientation by sponsoring a school wide reception and evening of fun for all the entering students.

Student activities. As long as the college operated on the crowded middle school campus the strategy had been for the Dean of Student's office to initiate the formation of a few societies and clubs. Activities had to be cleared with the middle school, since facilities were shared by the two schools. The staff in the Dean of Student's office usually initiated a series of school-wide events, like annual student day, Christmas parties, athletic meets, launch picnics, and the like, and utilized the society and club officers to get student participation.

After the move to the permanent campus student initiative in society and club activities picked up. Offices and other facilities were provided for the student officers. The strategy was to provide office facilities and limited funds for society and club use, and to exercise little staff control over the programs. With so many students more rigid control would have been difficult. Faculty sponsors usually were invited to attend affairs but were not asked to participate in plans. Since students knew that social dancing was not allowed on campus, a variety of games and more formal programs were provided. There was still little mixing of the sexes at these gatherings, although by now young people, especially those from the English language middle schools, were accustomed to more dating and other outward evidences of boy-girl interests and activities.

The Christian student organization had its own offices and active faculty sponsors. A separate budget was available to them. The student leaders developed and exercised more independence on the new campus. They tended to be less subservient to the faculty advisers. They promoted parties and receptions of their own and sought as many of the non-Christian students as possible.

Special-interest clubs, in addition to the department societies, proliferated on the new campus. In addition to the Dramatics Club, the Overseas Student Club, The Photographic Club, and the Fine Arts Club, which had been formed on the middle school campus, other groups as follows were organized:

> World University Service
> International Club
> Swimming and Hiking Groups
> A Table Tennis Club
> A Badminton Club
> Bowling Groups
> A Music Club
> Several Pop Musical Groups
> An Orchestra
> Several Choral Groups
> A Cinema Club
> A Chinese Art Club
> A Hostel Club

However, the Student Association and department societies, to one of which every student belonged, developed as the chief instruments for student social life. Largeness made for diversity of interests and plenty of students to compete in intercollegiate affairs in which the college usually fared well. In many respects student life and interest was highest of all on the campus of Hong Kong Baptist College.

In 1968 for the first time the Dean of Students was asked to enforce the rule that students whose academic records were below standard were not eligible to hold office in societies and clubs or participate on athletic teams. This was a strategy to control the growing number of students who neglected their studies for extra curricular activities. The academic quality of the school needed to be bolstered.

Student assemblies. Considerable experimentation was undertaken to make the assemblies, usually religious in nature, more effective. For one year they were scheduled at a noon hour, instead of mid-morning, but this proved to be a mistake. Since discipline became a serious problem in large groups the student body was first divided by Faculties for assemblies. It was discovered that attitudes of non-cooperation were more quickly learned by entering students when they mixed in this way with upperclassmen. Consequently, the decision was later made to separate new students from upperclassmen and to arrange programs designed for each separate group.

Beginning in 1966 each student attended only one assembly per week. The periods were shortened to thirty minutes, and speakers were limited to twelve minutes. This was a strategy to get better planned, fast moving programs as well as to conserve more time for class periods, and minimize student unrest and misbehavior.

Religious Emphasis Weeks. Special emphasis was given to religion one week each semester and this was quite acceptable to students. Much planning went into these programs, since the strategy was to make them outstanding semester events. A festive atmosphere was deliberately provided. The strategy of getting outstanding western and Chinese speakers, usually from outside Hong Kong, was augmented by bringing outstanding Christian Chinese movie stars or other entertainers to present special music or testimonies at the meetings. These added attractions made the meetings more interesting to Christian and non-Christian alike.

Founders' Day Services. Beginning with the 1962 session a Founders' Day special convocation was held, usually in March or April. The day included a morning service and suspension of classes. Special outings or athletic events were held in the afternoons, and social gatherings were in order for the evening. Occasional efforts to get graduates to attend special evening programs were successful.

Founders' Day programs emphasized educational rather than religious themes. Speakers represented a variety of groups, as Table XXII below shows.

TABLE XXII

HONG KONG BAPTIST COLLEGE
FOUNDERS' DAY SPEAKERS

Year	Speaker	Title
1962	Dr. J. Winston Crawley	Secretary for the Orient, Southern Baptist Mission Board
1963	Dr. C.T. Yung	President of Chung Chi College
1964	Dr. John W. Shepard	Chairman of the Japan Baptist Mission
1965	Rev. Loren Noren	Representative of the American Baptist Mission in Hong Kong
1966	Dr. David Y.K. Wong	One of the founders of the College and Chairman of the Board of Governors, 1956-68
1967	Dr. Edwin B. Dozier	Chancellor of Seinan Gakuin University, Fukuoka, Japan
1968	Mrs. Edgar Bates	Chairman of the Women's Department of the Baptist World Alliance, Ontario, Quebec, Canada

Classroom instruction. By the end of 1963 the required courses in Religion were revised. Thereafter, instead of offering Bible and Theology during the first three years, students were enrolled as follows:

1. Junior Division and Freshman   Christian Orientation and History of Religion
2. Sophomores   New Testament
3. Juniors   Old Testament
4. Seniors   Christian Philosophy and Ethics

The strategy was to appear to conform to the Director of Education's request that fewer courses in religion be required. Actually the first and last years' courses were treated as history and philosophy respectively. Another part of this strategy was to organize first year courses in such a way as to give students an understanding of the living religions of the world from the Christian viewpoint. It happened that the Chinese who lectured in Religion was especially versed in this subject and willing and able to take all freshmen students in several large classes. The instruction was in Chinese, and both economy and effectiveness were achieved. A third part of the strategy was to put the more difficult Old Testament course later than the New Testament course in the curriculum. A fourth part of the strategy was to offer Seniors a more sophisticated course with the possibility of a variety of approaches, depending on the availability of qualified teachers.

Early in the 1960's a strategy was pursued to inaugurate physical training and fine arts courses. Students were permitted to choose one elective course in Chinese art, dramatics and speech, or music, without extra charge. This maneuver provided the musical groups needed on public occasions and a dramatic group for fund-raising activity. The art classes exhibited their works each year. All of these activities were good for public relations and helped to project a good image in the community with very little expense to the school.

Laboratory insturction and field work in related courses took on greater proportions during this period. Efforts were made to keep up with developments in the Chinese University. In social work, students practiced side by side with students from the universities in agencies of the Colony. Field work training and supervision became major part of the curriculum.

In 1967 Education Department inspectors, some coopted from the universities, came to inspect the teaching program and to discuss curriculum and other matters with faculty and students. This was in connection with the college's application for Government approval for registration. Every effort was made to demonstrate the high quality of the teaching program.

Department heads and deans constantly reviewed course offerings and revised the curriculum of the respective departments. The tendency was to add courses. A struggle went on between those who favored more or less English and Chinese, as required courses. Seldom did a department head or dean question the required religion course, however. The strategy of giving department heads freedom in adding courses, brought expense, since courses tended to proliferate.

The Academic Board which met six times a year was the control center of the teaching program. These meetings gave unity, coherence, and guidance to the program of instruction.

Student dropout. The rate of student defection was high during this period for the same reasons as before. Obviously, ineligibility to grant degree was a major factor. Students who could not get into one of the universities or go abroad enrolled in the college. [9]   Many intended to go abroad after a year or two. [10] Some students were in the college temporarily to occupy their time, and consequently failure was common. Many poorly prepared students who matriculated in science would not otherwise have enrolled. Science teachers, aware of this fact, held a high standard in these classes and failed more students than they passed. [11] Many dropped out of school when they could not keep up.

Table XXIII below shows the percentage of students who matriculated in the five year period beginning 1960 and who graduated after the four year cycle.

TABLE XXIII

HONG KONG BAPTIST COLLEGE
RETENTION OF MATRICULATED FRESHMEN THROUGH
GRADUATION, 1960-64

Year	Number of Students Matriculated	Number who Graduated Four Years later	Percentage Retained
1960	258	98	38
1961	333	101	30
1962	409	102	25
1963	458	173	38
1964	505	161	32

Source: The office Records of the Registrar, Hong Kong Baptist College, 1960-68.

The graduates. The number and percentage of graduates by areas of spe-
cilizationa from 1960 through 1968 is shown in the Table XXIV. (page 123)

It can be seen, the most obvious changes were in the number and proportions of students majoring in engineering science. The general trend was downward until in 1968, when only 4 percent of the graduating class was in this area
of specialization. The proportion of those in business tended to rise. There was
considerable fluctuation up and down in arts and the physical sciences, with a
general upward trend in arts and downward trend in the physical sciences. The
social sciences maintained a stable percentage of graduates year by year.

Table XXV show the sex composition of the graduates of the college, 1960
to 1968. (page 124)

The trend was in the direction of a larger proportion of women graduates
in relation to men. On two occasions the number of women exceeded the number of men.

Table XXVI (page 124) shows the numbers and percentages of students
who graduated with distinction (2.0 quality point average or better), and who
just passed. (1.0 was the normative minimum for graduation) This table shows
that more students graduated with minimum standards than with distinction.
Beginning in 1964, students whose averages fell below 0.95 were required to do
special summer work before being presented diplomas later in September.[12]

Well over 15 percent of the graduates of Hong Kong Baptist College went
to universities abroad for further study. Most went to the United States,
Canada, and Australia. Many earned higher degrees and retained residence in the
West. Others are completing graduate studies. The majority of the remainder
are employed in Hong Kong. A few are self-employed, and over twenty are now
on the faculty and staff of the college. Only a few are active members of the
Alumni Association which holds membership in the Chinese Christian Universities Alumni Association. [13]

Major negative feedback from establishments and agencies employing graduates was with regards to their comparatively weak English. In general, they
were highly praised for their integrity and willingness to work hard and overtime
without complaint. They were in demand because many organizations could not

TABLE XXIV

HONG KONG BAPTIST COLLEGE GRADUATES
1960-68

Year	Arts		Social Sciences		Business		Physical Sciences		Engineering Sciences		Number of Major Areas	Total
	Number	Percent	Number	Percent	Number	Percent	Number	Percent	Number	Percent		
1960	4	6	18	27	6	9	9	14	29	44	5	66
1961	11	11	26	27	25	26	12	12	23	24	5	97
1962	9	9	22	21	22	22	26	25	24	23	6	103
1963	23	19	21	18	30	26	19	16	25	21	10	118
1964	22	22	22	22	31	30	14	14	12	12	11	101
1965	15	15	29	29	26	25	19	19	13	12	11	102
1966	9	9	22	22	35	35	24	23	13	13	11	103
1967	40	23	35	20	40	24	28	16	30	17	12	173
1968	41	25	35	22	59	36	21	13	7	4	13	163
TOTAL	174	17	230	22	274	27	172	17	176	17		1,026

Source: Office Records of the Registrar, 1960-68.

TABLE XXV

HONG KONG BAPTIST COLLEGE
SEX OF GRADUATES, 1960-68

Year	Total Number	Male	Percent	Female	Percent
1960	66	46	62	20	30
1961	99	59	60	40	40
1962	110	65	59	45	41
1963	117	61	52	56	48
1964	98	45	46	53	54
1965	101	58	57	43	43
1966	102	55	54	47	46
1967	173	81	47	92	53
1968	161	100	62	61	38

Source: The Registrar's Office Records, 1960-68.

TABLE XXVI

HONG KONG BAPTIST COLLEGE
GRADUATES WITH DISTINCTION AND GRADUATES WITH
THE MINIMUM STANDARD, 1960-68

Year	Total Number	Number with Distinction	Percentage	Number with Minimum Grade	Percentage
1960	66	11	18	15	23
1961	99	17	17	27	28
1962	110	11	10	19	17
1963	117	11	9	23	20
1964	98	11	11	19	19
1965	101	7	7	26	26
1966	102	6	6	27	26
1967	173	11	6	27	16
1968	161	19	12	24	15

Source: Registrar's Office Records, 1960-68.

afford to pay salaries expected by the University graduates, and the college graduates were willing to work for less.

STRATEGIES DESIGNED TO WORK OUT
PUBLIC RELATIONS PROBLEMS

Alignments. Apart from the Hong Kong-Macau Baptist Mission, and its parent body, the Foreign Mission Board in the United States, and the Hong Kong Baptist Association, the college officials have not found alignments for substantial support. This is at least partially true because no strategy has been followed to that end.

Government alignments for indirect subsidy never developed. Requests for outright money grants or loans were submitted but turned down. Consequently, the college officials again pursued registration under the Post-secondary Ordinance.

In 1967 representatives of the United Board for Higher Education in Asia included the college in an Asia-wide survey (referred to in Chapter 1), and suggested that the college should seek other sources of support. The Constitution makes provision for the appointment of several Board members provided they have the approval of the Association Executive Committee, but no concrete move has been made to coopt outsiders on the governing board.

An effort has been made to get financial help from a number of American foundations. Several gifts of money, mainly for the building program came from one of them, but no regular source of support was found.

The establishment of a Department of Communication in 1968 was encouraged by Asia Foundation representatives in Hong Kong, and had the endorsement of several local organizations like the Far East Broadcasting Company. It had some help from that organization in the way of personnel on the teaching staff which came through a loosely structured agreement. The founder of the American-based Laubach Literacy Foundation came to the college staff in 1967-68. An exchange professor from San Francisco State College was at the college for the 1968-69 session. The college officials however, are guided by no clear cut policy to move firmly and realisticly in the direction of establishing meaningful alignments beyond present Association and Baptist Mission Board arrangements.

Publicity. Forward steps in publicity have been taken beyond those of the first four year cycle of operation. One strategy has been to bring outstanding Hong Kong and American elites to speak at Commencement occasions. Table XXVII below shows the success which has been achieved in this respect. Another strategy has been to improve the quality of newspaper and magazine publicity and to project a truer image of the college. The strategy has unfolded in the telling of the story of the college's dynamic development.

TABLE XXVII

SPEAKERS AT HONG KONG BAPTIST COLLEGE
COMMENCEMENT, 1960-68

Year	Name	Position
1960	Dr. W.R. White	President, Baylor University, Waco, Texas
1961	Dr. Paul Stevens	Director, Southern Baptist Radio and Television Commission, Fort Worth, Texas
1962	Sir Robert Black	Governor of Hong Kong
1963	Dr. John Raley	President, Oklahoma Baptist University, Shawnee, Oklahoma
1964	Dr. Baker James Cauthen	Executive Secretary, Foreign Mission Board, Southern Baptist Convention, Richmond, Virginia
1965	Dr. John A. Hunter	President, Louisiana State University, Baton Rouge, Louisiana
1966	Dr. F.E. Wright	President, Union University, Jefferson City, Tennessee
1967	Prof. K.E. Robinson	Vice Chancellor, University of Hong Kong
1968	The Honorable William Gregg	Director of Education, Hong Kong

Source: Records in the Office of the Vice President, 1960-68.

The college's own news magazine has a striking format and good coverage with action pictures. It is published and mailed to a growing list of friends and organizations in Hong Kong and overseas. Releases to the Chinese and English-language newspapers in Hong Kong have been better coordinated by the Office for College Relations and Development.

Television and radio have been utilized, with four of the leading radio and television headquarters located now in the general area of Kowloon as is the college. The strategy of the college is to develop a strong Communication Department which will link it with leading local communication networks. It expects to utilize some of their experts on the teaching staff and in an advisory capacity. Graduates from the department who find employment in mass media organizations are expected to strengthen the links.

The most spectacular success in publicity was the appearance of a full page advertisement of the college in the January, 1968, issue of the Asian version of Time Magazine. [14]

Fund-raising. Funds to erect the building and equip the new campus were received for the most part since 1960. Table XXVIII (page 129) itemizes income for building and equipment received through 1966, and expenditures.

The formal opening of the college campus in October, 1966 was a well-planned occasion and attracted many guests. The Governor of Hong Kong and the Executive Secretary of the Southern Baptist Foreign Mission Board, [15] along with the Board officials and College administrators, and other distinguished guests, were on the program.

Since the opening of the building the repayment of the Pui Ching Middle School and the Foreign Mission Board loans have been put into the operating budget of the college. A fund-raiser, referred to in the earlier section, was employed, but his services were not continued after 1967. The college authorities again sought a Government interest-free loan to improve the facilities without success. Recently the remainder of the large loan due to be paid back during three more years to the Foreign Mission Board was made as a contribution to the college. Thus, the indebtedness is no longer a burden.

WHAT'S NEW IN HONG KONG?

Hong Kong Baptist College? *Well, not quite as new as Plover Cove Dam (only one-third full as yet). But just as urgent. Probably more so. Asian students are desperate for education, in case you haven't noticed.*

Actually, we were founded in 1956. But don't consider us old-hat. We just haven't had time to get into the conventional academic rut. Last year we moved into our new campus—all 1800 of us. The most modern in Hong Kong, by the way. Next year, to our twelve major areas of study, we shall add a Colony first—our Department of Communications. Dr. Frank C. Laubach, the internationally known each-one-teach-one specialist, joined us this fall to offer a special Literacy Journalism class.

We're young and brash enough to try new things in our effort to be contemporary and to fit into the unique environment which is Hong Kong. We teach a course in interviewing, for instance, and one in practical social work (the students work under supervision in established organizations).

And, of course, the expected ones—Chinese language and literature, foreign languages and literature, history, geography, biology, chemistry,

mathematics, physics, civil engineering, business administration, accountancy and secretarial studies.

You might say that we are trilingual—we teach in Cantonese, Mandarin and English. Impossible? Perhaps. But then Asian students are rather unusual. With the academic world at large, we are engaged in the quest for truth. But more. We believe that truth can be found and in turn requires a commitment from us.

Hong Kong Baptist College is committed to the Christian view of man and society and accepts the social responsibility that goes with this view. We don't claim to understand all that this means, but we are interested in finding out. If you share our concern, we invite your inquiries and support.

For further information, please write to:

The Office of College Relations and Development,
Hong Kong Baptist College,
224, Waterloo Road, Kowloon, Hong Kong.

HONG KONG BAPTIST COLLEGE,

Waterloo Road, Kowloon, Hong Kong.

President: Dr. Lam Chi-Fung.   Vice-President: Dr. Maurice J. Anderson.

ILLUSTRATION 7
A free advertisement in the Asian edition of Time Magazine, January, 1968

TABLE XXVIII

HONG KONG BAPTIST COLLEGE
RECEIPTS AND DISBURSEMENTS FOR THE NEW CAMPUS
UP TO MARCH, 1967

Receipts

Donations, Local		$1,508,236.00	
Donations, South East Asia		231,810.00	
Donations, U.S.A.			
Building Funds	$3,843,236.00		
Miscellaneous Gifts, 1966	141,000.00		
Foreign Mission Board subsidy	70,000.00		
Equipment Funds	494,557.00	4,548,793.00	$6,288,839.00
Interest Income		30,000.00	
Miscellaneous Income		54,788.00	
Accumulated excess of Income		54,212.00	109,000.00
over expenditure from general			
operating, 1956-66			201,957.00
Loans:			
Foreign Mission Board		860,625.00	
Pui Ching Middle School		241,283.00	
Student Deposits (temporarily		100,000.00	1,201,908.00
borrowed)			$7,801,704.00

Expenditures

Building and Grounds:		
Site Formation	$1,614,460.00	
Architect Fees	348,399.00	
Building Construction	4,260,127.00	
Installation and Equipment	337,340.00	
Track and Field	28,098.00	
Miscellaneous	39,627.00	$6,628,051.00
Furniture, Fixtures and Equipment:		
Furniture and Fixtures	$ 571,156.00	
Reference Books	140,192.00	
Laboratory Equipment	424,155.00	
Library Equipment	16,536.00	
Miscellaneous	21,614.00	1,173,653.00
		$7,801,704.00

Source: Office of the Accountant, Hong Kong Baptist College.

ANALYSES AND CONCLUSIONS

An analysis of the Hong Kong Baptist College system, now a full scale competitive complex organizaiotn, can be made as follows.

General System Characteristics

Importation of Energy. During the period from 1960-1968 it was necessary for the Hong Kong Baptist College system to rely heavily on resources outside itself. The descriptions given earlier indicate that "energy" was imported in terms of (1) funds raised, (2) land acquired, (3) facilities and equipment obtained, (4) staff and faculty recruited, (5) development of teaching and training programs, (6) student recruitment procedures perfected, (7) and public relations worked out.

Throughput. After the move to the new premises in 1966 student clubs proliferated as did athletic, music and ohter special interest groups. Departmental societies functioned with many more activities. The Student Association was formed and began to be an active force in the throughput. Laboratory courses, field work, and classroom instruction took on the features associated with a serious academic undertaking. Students identified better with the school. All these are examples of improved throughput, as is the higher academic level developed.

Output. Eight sets of students, more than 1,000 in all, graduated from the school by July, 1968. Not until 1967 did the output show considerable increase over previous years. The above phenomenon was looked upon by school authorities as beneficial to the system, since the employment market was not flooded, and there continued to be a ready demand for the graduates. The quality of the graduates, judged by such measures as academic achievement, was about the same every year.

Cycle of events. During the period the cycles of events in all levels of the structure took on regular patterns. Several events intended to be regularized never got firmly established, however. The faculty journal, for instance, which should have been issued annually became a reality only three times in the nine years period.

Many students failed to complete the cycle as programmed in four years.

for them college become a five year cycle. Also, one set of students beginning in 1967, was admitted to a five year period of study. They took their university preparatory course at the Baptist College.

Negative entropy. The Governors and college officials acted energetically to get funds to erect and equip the college buildings. Since the system operated in borrowed space for its first ten years, such activity was essential for the healthy state and survival of a college without a campus.

When the Hong Kong Government subsidized three competitor schools and assisted them to become foundation colleges of the Chinese University, much energy was spent to contact the sources of power for similar legitimation. Teachers and staff sensed the competitive situation and improved the quality of their performance. So much energy was generated by so many actors both in getting material resources and in improving the functioning of the organization that a steady development process continued.

The differentiationof areas of specialization was also in the interest of a healthy state. The system was able thereby to adjust to community needs and to innovate with new departments and courses, and put out graduates needed in the outside environment.

Negative feedback. Employment of the graduates in industrial, business, architectural, and engineering firms, social welfare agencies, schools, and church organizations, resulted in considerable feedback year by year. Chief criticism were that graduates' English standards was weak, and they did not know how to conduct themselves in interviews with prospective employers, it was said. As a result teachers insisted on more intensive use of speech laboratories and modern teaching techniques, and specialists came to the school to instruct students in how to behave in interviews with prospective employers.

Differentiation. The departments of instruction were differentiated into Faculties of Arts and Science in the early 1960's. In 1965 further differentiation into three faculties, with a new Faculty of Business, followed. New departments such as History and Geography, Chinese, Secretarial Studies, and Communication were added.

Early in the 1960's heads were appointed for teaching departments. The choice of personnel also was more and more in terms of specialized teaching needs.

Steady state. Authorities were alert to keep the college program balanced. The input and dropout of students continued to be a major concern. Care was taken to keep correspondence current with donors abroad. Strains in sub-units of the system were watched. Much of the energy which may have been directed toward energetic input and improvement of the training porcess, however, was expended in strategies to ease tension.

Equifinality. Changes in curriculum and teacher turnover had some effect on the student product. During the early years of operation, for instance, many majored in mathematics. When several teachers resigned in the early 1960's *en masse* the emphasis changed to chemistry. Changing trends as to departments of specialization continued during this whole period.

Behavioral Stress during the Period of Competitive Operation

Years of continuing operation in crowded Pui Ching Middle School provided for the behavioral stress outlined in Chapter VII. After the move to a permanent campus other major stress situations arose.

The Board of Governors. By 1966 missionaries on the Board sensed that the control of the college was so dominated by one power constellation that the situation provided them little facility to take the fole of Governor. Furthermore, the cultural differences between East and West began to be more in evidence. The overpowering leadership style of the Chinese administrator also frustrated most Board members, Chinese and western, so that little activity outside of the inner circle of relatives and obligated officers was in evidence. Participation in Board interaction became more and more limited and may be largely attributed to role frustration due to a situation which did not facilitate action of most of the members.

The Administration. The incongruous situation of a western Vice President for all practical purposes in charge of the college changed to some extent after the move to the new campus. The President thereafter functioned as the head of the organization. However, diverse expectations brought by easterners and westerners to administrative roles were more in evidence in the new setting. Personality styles of the now six to eight actors in administration also complicated interaction and brought more stress than before. The frustration felt by all was intensified by the fact that formal interaction situations were not conducive to mutual trust and confidence in which all were willing to express themselves openly. The administrators were also in stress since none seemed to have a clear understanding of how he was expected to function. The person now in charge seemed to treat these elites in a way that would be more appropriate in relations with staff in a business firm or a secondary school. The centrality of power rather than its diffusion and clearcut delegation was in evidence.

Restructuring of the administrative unit took place when Board officers set up regular meetings with the President and the western Vice President and Comptroller for discussion and decision. This helped to alleviate some of the frustration which the East-West mixture, coupled with a variety of personality styles among the administrators, had precipitated. Doubtless incongruity due to the fact that some persons still had to function without the positive sanctions which go with responsibility continued to be a source of strain.

The staff. Many of the Chinese staff found themselves unprepared to function in their roles on the new campus. The rapid enlargement of the student body put heavier loads of work on each of them than before. Instalation of modern equipment rather than addition of staff added to their sense of inadequacy. This brought added frustration, since their office arrangements had to be reorganized and new procedures had to be learned. The employment of new staff on the basis of family connections and friendship rather than skill and efficiency brought more frustration to managers who then had additional inadequate help but no facility to control or get rid of them.

Fortunately, many of the officers had efficient managers, either Chinese or western, and activity continued with a minimum of frustration. Mainly in the Business and Registrar's offices, where data processing equipment was introduced in 1968 was staff stress most evident. Faculty and student contacts with these officers for financial and classroom arrangements were frequent and provided most of the situations of stress.

The faculty. Many faculty members during this period also served as deans and department heads, while at the same time continuing to carry heavy teaching loads. These persons were often in role conflict due to the division of their time between teaching and administration. They had limited opportunities to be efficient in either role.

A rapid turnover of faculty personnel made possible the employment of young Chinese just out of graduate schools in the West. They were motivated professionally to maintain high teaching standards but had to teach large classes and advanced subjects for which they had little time to prepare. The situation did not facilitate the individual attention which students expected and produced role frustration.

A large number of westerners and Chinese all new to Hong Kong Baptist College were on teaching staffs together. Their interaction was often frustrated by differing cultural expectations brought to the teaching role. Their newness to the college as well as little experience in interaction as fellow teachers with persons of diverse cultural backgrounds also made it difficult for them to function as a team in departmental settings. Westerners most of whom did not understand Chinese found themselves in meetings and discussion situations in which they could not interact at all. On the other hand, when meetings were conducted in English some of the Chinese teachers failed to interact, since they did not understand what was being said. Both role frustration and non-reciprocity developed because of the unusual language and other cultural factors which necessarily complicated interaction.

Students. Many students were frustrated before they came to the college because they failed to get into one of the universities in Hong Kong or elsewhere. They were students at Hong Kong Baptist College more out of necessity than by choice.

Large classes and improper room assignments at the college brought frustration to some who had to stand during class at the beginning of the session until adjustments were made. Mistakes by office personnel in assigning and scheduling of courses also brought stress to many during the first weeks of school.

Different expectations of western and Chinese teachers with regard to classroom performance, examinations, and interpersonal relations brought stress to students. Since there were more new western and Chinese teachers during this period this kind of frustration was more common than during the earlier period.

The cultural structure, personality factors and the situation in which they found themselves cohtributed to student stress, mainly in the form of role frustration. Fortunately, the majority were able to adjust by accepting and becoming accustomed to the college situation or by going elsewhere. Most of those who remained in school found college life quite satisfying, especially in their Junior and Senior years.

---

1. From Registrar's Office Records.
2. Hong Kong Baptist College Bulletin, 1966-68, pp. 16-17.
3. From Hong Kong Baptist College Statement of Accounts, 1966-67, Lowe, Bigham, and Matthews, chartered accountants.
4. See Appendix B for the salary scale which went into effect in 1966.
5. See Appendix D for a copy of Conditions of Service given to each employee of the college.
6. From Records in the Office of the Registrar, 1960-63.
7. The writer conducted the survey by means of a questionnaire.
8. The writer also conducted the survey by means of a questionnaire.
9. A survey of students by the Dean of Studies in 1964 showed that at least half of those who enrolled tried to get into one of the universities or intended to go abroad as soon as possible.
10. A faculty poll in 1967 showed that many believed the college should serve as a 'stepping stone' to get to an American university.
11. A study of teachers' grading patterns in 1966 by the writer revealed that failures in basic science courses were much higher than other basic courses in the faculties of Arts or Business. American consulate authorities who interviewed students going abroad often said a 'C' grade in Science was equivalent to a 'B' in Arts or Business.
12. Academic Board Meeting Minutes, July 3, 1961, June 29, 1962, June 25, 1963, June 29, 1964, June 28, 1965, July 1, 1966, June 28, 1967, and June 26, 1968.
13. This organization is a federation of thirteen Chinese Christian University Alumni Associations, the Association of Chung Chi College Alumni and the Hong Kong Baptist College Alumni Association.
14. Illustration 7, page 128. A fund-raiser, Mr. Winston McClellon of North Carolina, worked for the college in 1967 and was instrumental in getting this free advertisement. The Consultant for College Relations and Development prepared the material.
15. His Excellency, Sir David Trench, Governor of Hong Kong, formally opened the building. Dr. Baker James Cauthen, Southern Baptist Foreign Mission Board Executive Secretary, came from Richmond, Virginia to deliver the main address.

CHAPTER IX

SUMMARY AND CONCLUSIONS

This exploratory case-study of a western-type educational religious complex organization has succeeded to some extent in achieving the purposes for which it was undertaking By pin-pointing the strategies of western and Chinese actors to found and operate the college the writer was able to "spell out" some of the processes of cooperation, competition, accommodation, conflict and confrontation which appeared. It became clear, as the analysis proceeded, that different expectations of actors from two diverse cultural groups, when brought into the interaction of administrators especially, and all actors to a lesser extent, was a potent source of stress in the structure of an organization. The more diverse these cultural backgrounds due to factors like the generation gap, education, and previous socialization, the more likely the stress might eventually lead to an unhealthy organizational state.

The analysis covers a period of approximately fifteen years and shows how the school organization changed. It was at first a comparatively small and simple system characterized by primary group relationships. It came to be a large, modern, complex, differentiated and more sophisticated association in which many interacted in secondary group relationships instead. The above also had an effect on the style of administrative control which was desirable. The direction of change should be toward more rationality. Efficiency of operation and open channels of communication up and down and across hierarchical lines of control must be maintained.

In the Hong Kong Baptist College the change from western to Chinese control in day to day administration was necessary when the college became fully competitive and was domiciled on its own campus. However, it was a mistake for this change to take the direction of less rationality in management and control.

Certainly the analysis made shows that stress and strain develop as actors are engaged in a common task and are brought together in more frequent and meaningful interaction. The differing expectations of western and Chinese staff at all levels of the structure, as well as differences among Chinese due to cultural, personality, and situational factors, and the interaction process itself, made stress a normal organizational feature. The writer was an actor in the administrative unit and probably interacted more frequently with Chinese administrators than other structural units. He thus was able to detect the stress in that unit of the structure more readily. However, he was in a position to interact also with faculty, staff, and students over a long period of time and did not experience the intensity of strain with them that he experienced with actors in administration. Probably interaction and communication in authority and power relationships brings more stress than in the other processes of college operation.

The modern "open" system model functioned as an adequate analytical tool, when the characteristics of such a system were the focus of the analysis. The model made possible the analysis of those features of a college organization which are of vital concern to administrators. The latter are more likely to be engaged in actions to get resources for successful input, throughput, and output and to keep the system in a healthy state than to pursue goals arbitrarily set by themselves or others. Such mundane matters as faculty selection, their status-position in departmental groups and their situses in the organization are concerns of administrators on which the model focuses. The organizational need to keep boundaries open and communication channels operative inside the structure and with the environment is pin-pointed by the use of this system model. The "loose" fit which is possible for the structural units of the organization can be shown by the use of the model. The process of change always goes on as organization, disorganization, and reorganization processes are articulated. A kind of homeostatis can be seen when input exceeds output. The model also demonstrates that products are not dependent on a rigid systematic throughput. In the process of training the college system tended to produce an end-product similar in many ways regardless of changes in throughput. Neither did it matter if the changes were deliberate or if they were happenings in the environment over which the system actors had no control.

The behavioral model was useful to account for and explain sources of tension in the college structure. By conceptualizing the four variables, the cultural structure, personality, the situation, and social interaction; maladjustment could be explained as stresses within the cultural structure or between the cultural structure and personality, a situation, or social interaction. The major stresses due to role conflict and role incongruity, role inadequacy, role frustration and role non-reciprocity could also be identified in the various units of the college structure.

Role conflict among members of the Board of Governors was due to incompatible norms perceived as obligations. Both missionaries and Chinese in these status-positions were in stress, and eventually only the few who did not experience exceptional strain functioned meaningfully. This meant that only a few, who were by ties of blood and friendship in intimate personal relations with the associational and college leader, were able to function actively on the Board. Role inadequacy among Board members was due in part to the limited numbers of persons in the Association and Mission eligible for election.

Role conflict between the western and Chinese administrators developed because the expectations which each brought to his situs in the organization were not compatible. The more they interacted without the niceties of East-West symbolic recognition of differences, the more intense was the stress. Role incongruity was present when the persons taking organizational responsibilities did not receive the positive sanctions which should go with responsibility.

Conflict was not great between Chinese and western staff partly because much of the work of specialists required little decision-making interaction. When such conflict did occur it was largely due to differing expectations due to the diverse cultures which each brought to his or her position in the group where interaction was most necessary. Conflict between Chinese staff members was due mainly to personality styles, interaction related to maladjustments in the administrative structure and the physical conditions which made Chinese actors unable to perform as expected.

Role inadequacy in the staff was largely due to the eastern practice of allocating positions on the basis of friendship and family. This was not dysfunctional at first because actors could be trained for the positions. However, the complex organization which had developed by the end of the 1960's, with a

large student body to be serviced, needed staff with office skills and bureaucratic efficiency. The new situation was frustrating to conscientious workers who
wanted to accomplish their tasks but did not know how to use the modern
equipment provided.

Faculty stress was mainly in the form of role frustration. In the borrowed
premises of the middle school inadequate space and facilities became more and
more in evidence as the student body grew, and this was the chief source of
strain. On the new campus the teacher-student ratio which was already high
continued to rise. Teachers were harassed with large classes and too many
students. With rapid teacher turnover and frequent student dropout the teaching
process became a source of frustration. The leftist distrubances in 1967 brought
stress to many who were devoted to the school. For the sake of their family
well-being and secuirty they left the Colony for more secure living conditions.

Student stress was mainly in the form of role frustration. After a year or
so in the Hong Kong Baptist College those who could left to attend colleges
where degrees were granted. Many who had gotten in with inadequate educational preparation were motivated to succeed in their college studies. However,
low grades and the danger of failure which was "face losing" among friends and
relatives brought frustration to many.

The following conclusions are derived from the analysis of the behavioral
stresses in the organization. (1) A broader base of material support for the Hong
Kong Baptist College should be sought, and representation on the Board of
Governors must reflect this base. (2) Each Chinese and western administrator
should have a clearer position description and should be given the positive sanctions which go with the responsibilities he takes in the organization. (3) Staff
appointments should be made on the basis of competence to assure efficiency
and economy in the operation of such a modern complex school system. (4) A
tenure system and a retirement plan for faculty and staff should be put into
operation. (5) If high academic achievement is a goal of the school, a teacher-
student ratio comparable to that required by American accrediting associations
must be maintained. A small student enrollment will enhance the teaching
and training goals for which the college was established.

Finally, actors from diverse cultural backgrounds in western-type organizations in the East should have definite orientation and briefing in characteristics
of both cultures before assuming roles in them. This would prepare them for the
peculiar nature of interactional demands on them in such settings.

BIBLIOGRAPHY

A. BOOKS

Abegglen, J.C. *The Japanese Factory: Aspects of its Social Organization.* Glencoe, Illinois: The Free Press, 1958.

Adorno, T.W., Else Frenkel-Brunswik, D.J. Levinson, and R.N. Sanford. *The Authoritarian Personality.* New York: Harper and Row Publishers, 1950.

Ahmad, J. *The Expert and the Administrator.* Pittsburg: University of Pittsburg, 1959.

An Appraisal of the Protestant Christian Effort in Higher Education in Asia: Hong Kong. An unpublished report. New York: The United Board for Higher Education in Asia, 1968.

Argyris, C. *Personality and Organization.* New York: Harper and Row Publishers, 1957.

Aron, Raymond. *Main Currents in Sociological Thought.* New York: Basic Books, Inc., 1965.

Bales, Robert F., Talcott Parsons, and Edward A. Shils. *Working Papers in the Theory of Action.* Glencoe, Illinois: The Free Press, 1953.

————, and Talcott Parsons. *Family, Socialization, and Interaction Process.* Glencoe, Illinois: The Free Press, 1955.

Banton, Michael (ed.). *The Social Anthropology of Complex Societies.* London: Tavistock Publications, 1966.

Barnard, Chester I. *The Functions of the Executive.* Cambridge: Harvard University Press, 1948.

Barton, Otomar J. *Simple Models of Group Behavior.* New York: Columbia University Press, 1967.

Bass, B.M. *Leadership, Psychology, and Organizational Behavior.* New York: Harper and Row Publishers, 1960.

Baufield, E. *The Moral Bases of a Backward Society.* Glencoe, Illinois: The Free Press, 1958.

Becker, Howard. *Boys in White.* Chicago: University of Chicago Press, 1961.

Bendix, R. *Max Weber, An Intellectual Portrait.* Garden City, New York: Doubleday, 1960.

———. *Work and Authority in Industry.* New York: John Wiley and Sons, Inc., 1956.

Bennett, John W., and Melvin M. Tumin. *Social Life, Structure and Function.* New York: Alfred A. Knopf, 1948.

Bertalanffy, Ludwig von. *Modern Theories of Development.* New York: Harper and Row, Publishers, Torchlight edition, 1962.

Bertrand, Alvin L. *Basic Sociology: An Introduction to Theory and Method.* New York: Appleton-Century-Crofts, 1967.

Biddle, Bruce J., and Erwin J. Thomas (eds.). *Role Theory: Concepts and Research.* New York: John Wiley and Sons, Inc., 1966.

Blackwell, Thomas E. *College and University Administration.* New York: The Center for applied Research in Education, Inc., 1966.

Blau, Peter M. *Bureaucracy in Modern Society.* New York: Random House, 1956.

———, and W. Richard Scott. *Formal Organization.* San Francisco: Chandler Publishing Company, 1962.

Blumer, Herbert. *An Appraisal of Thomas and Znaniecki's "The Polish Peasant in Europe and America."* New York: Social Science Research Council, 1939.

Bruyn, Severyn T. *The Human Perspective in Sociology: The Methodology of Participant Observation.* Englewood Cliffs, New Jersey: Prentice-Hall, Inc., 1966.

Buckley, Walter. *Sociology and Modern System Theory.* Englewood Cliffs, New Jersey: Prentice-Hall, Inc., 1967.

Caplow, Theodore. *Principles of Organization.* New York: Harcourt, Brace, and World, 1964.

Chai, Ch'u and Winberg Chai. *The Changing Society of China.* New York: The New American Library of World Literature, Inc., 1962.

Chinoy, Ely. *Sociological Perspectives.* New York: Random House, Inc., 1954.

Chow, K.R. *The Hong Kong Economy.* Hong Kong: Economic Research Center, The Chinese University of Hong Kong, 1966.

Clark, Burton R. *The Open Door College: A Case Study.* New York: McGraw-Hill Book Company, Inc., 1960.

Coleman, J.S. *The Adolescent Society.* Glencoe, Illinois: The Free Press, 1961.

Corson, John J. *Governance of Colleges and Universities.* New York: McGraw-Hill Book Company, 1960.

Coser, L.A. *The Function of Social Conflict.* Glencoe, Illinois: The Free Press, 1956.

Davis, Kingsley. *Human Society.* New York: The Macmillan Company, 1949.

Durkheim, Emile. *The Division of Labor in Society.* Translated by George Simpson. Glencoe, Illinois: The Free Press, 1947.

———, *Education adn Sociology.* Translated by S.D. Fox. Glencoe, Illinois: The Free Press, 1956.

———. *Suicide.* Translated by George Simpson. Glencoe, Illinois: The Free Press, 1951.

Ehrlich, Howard J. *An Examination of Role Theory.* Lincoln, Nebraska: University of Nebraska Press, 1966.

Etzioni, Amatai. *A Comparative Analysis of Complex Organizations.* Glencoe, Illinois: The Free Press, 1961.

_____(ed.). *Complex Organizations, A Sociological Reader.* New York: Holt, Rinehart, and Winston, Inc., 1961.

Faculty Participation in Academic Governance. A report of the American Association for Higher Education. Washington, D.C.: American Association for Higher Education, 1967.

Fallding, Harold. *The Sociological Task.* Englewood Cliffs, New Jersey: Prentice-Hall, Inc., 1968.

Fallers, L.A. *Bantu Bureaucracy.* Cambridge, England: W. Heffer, 1956.

Festinger, Leon and Daniel Katz. *Research Methods in the Behavioral Sciences.* New York: Holt, Rinehart, and Winston, 1953.

Fichter, Joseph S., S.J. *The Parochical School: A Sociological Study.* Notre Dame, Indiana: Notre Dame University Press, 1958.

_____. *Social Relations in the Urban Parish.* Chicago: University of Chicago Press, 1954.

Firth, Raymond. *Elements of Social Organization.* Boston: Beacon Press, 1961.

Frazier, Franklin. *Race and Culture Contacts in the Modern World.* Boston: Beacon Press, 1957.

Gerth, H.H., and C.W. Mills. *From Max Weber.* New York: Oxford University Press, 1946.

Gordon, C. Wayne. *The Social System of the High School.* Glencoe, Illinois: The Free Press, 1957.

Gouldner, Alvin W. *Patterns of Industrial Bureaucracy.* Glencoe, Illinois: The Free Press, 1955.

Grannick, D. *Management of the Industrial Firm in the U.S.S.R.* New York: Columbia University Press, 1954.

_____. *The Red Executive: A Study of the Organization Man in Russian Industry.* Garden City, New York: Doubleday, 1960.

Gross, Nea., Ward S. Mason, and Alexander W. McEachern. *Explorations in Role Analysis.* New York: John Wiley and Sons, Inc., 1966.

Haire, Mason (ed.). *Modern Organization Theory.* New York: John Wiley and Sons, Inc., 1959.

Hiller, E.T. *Social Relations and Structure.* New York: Harper and Brothers, 1947.

Hollingshead, A.B. *Elmtown's Youth.* New York: John Wiley and Sons, Inc., 1949.

Homans, George C. *The Human Group.* New York: Harcourt, Brace, and World, Inc., 1950.

Hopkins, Terence K. *The Exercise of Influence in Small Groups.* Totowa, New Jersey: The Bedminster Press, 1964.

Jacob, P. *Changing Values in College.* New York: Harper and Row Publishers, 1957.

Janowitz, M. *Sociology and the Military Establishment.* New York: Russell Sage Foundation, 1959.

Kahn, Robert L. and Elsie Boulding (eds.). *Power and Conflict in Organizations.* New York: Basic Books, Inc., 1964.

Katz, Daniel and Robert L. Kahn. *The Social Psychology of Organization.* New York: John Wiley and Sons, Inc., 1966.

Kretch, D. and R.S. Crutchfield. *Theory and Problems of Social Psychology.* New York: McGraw-Hill Book Comapny, 1948.

LaPiere, Richard T. and Paul R. Farnsworth. *Social Psychology*. Third Edition. New York: McGraw-Hill Book Company, 1949.

Lazarsfeld, Paul F., and Wagner J. Thielens. *The Academic Mind*. Glencoe, Illinois: The Free Press, 1958.

_____, and Morris Rosenberg. *The Language of Social Research*. Glencoe, Illinois: The Free Press, 1955.

Lenski, Gerhard. *Power and Privilege: A Theory of Social Stratification*. New York: McGraw-Hill Book Company, 1966.

Levy, Marion. *The Structure of Society*. Princeton, New Jersey: Princeton University Press, 1952.

Li, Chien Nung. *The Political History of China*, 1840-1928. New York: Van Nostrand, 1963.

Likert, Rensis. *New Patterns of Management*. New York: McGraw-Hill Book Company, 1961.

Lindzey, Gardner. *Handbook of Social Psychology*. Reading, Massachusetts: Addison-Wesley Publishing Company, Inc., 1954.

Litterer, Joseph A. (ed.). *Organizations, Structure, and Behavior*. New York: John Wiley and Sons, Inc., 1963.

Loomis, Charles P. *Social Systems*. Princeton, New Jersey: D. Van Nostrand, 1960.

Lynd, Robert S. and Hellen Merrell Lynd. *Middletown*. New York: Harcourt, Brace, and Company, 1929.

Malinowski, B. *Crime and Custom in Savage Society*. New York: Harcourt, Brace, and Company, 1926.

March, J.G. and H. Simon. *Handbook of Organizations*. New York: John Wiley and Sons, Inc., 1958.

Martindale, Don. *Institutions, Organizations, and Mass Society*. Boston: Houghton Mifflin Company, 1966.

_____. *Social Life and Cultural Change*. New York: D. Van Nostrand Company, Inc., 1962.

McGrath, Earl J. (ed.). *Selected Issues in College Administration*. New York: Teachers College Press, Columbia University, 1967.

McKinney, John C. *Constructive Typology and Social Theory*. New York: Appleton-Century-Crofts, 1966.

Merton, Robert. *Social Theory and Social Structure*. Enlarged edition. New York: The Free Press, 1968.

Millett, John D. *The Academic Community, An Essay on Organization*. New York: McGraw-Hill Book Company, Inc., 1962.

Mitchell, William. *Sociological Analysis and Politics: The Theories of Talcott Parsons*. Englewood, New Jersey: Prentice-Hall, Inc., 1967.

Mott, Paul E. *The Organization of Society*. Englewood Cliffs, New Jersey: Prentice-Hall, Inc., 1965.

Nadel, F. *The Theory of Social Structure*. Glencoe, Illinois: The Free Press, 1956.

Newcomb, T.M. *Personality and Social Change*. New York: The Dryden Press, 1943.

Northrop, F. S.C. *Meeting of the East and West*. Second Edition. New York: Collier-Macmillan Company, 1966.

Olsen, Marvin E. *The Process of Social Organization*. New York: Holt, Rinehart, and Winston, 1968

Pang, S.H. *The Needs of Hong Kong, 1957*. Les Rasses, Switzerland, 1958.

Parsons, Talcott. *Social System*. Glencoe, Illinois: The Free Press, 1950.

Parsons, Talcott. *Structure and Process in Modern Societies*. Glencoe, Illinois: The Free Press, 1960.

_____, and E.A. Shils. *Toward a General Theory of Action*. Cambridge, Massachusetts: Harvard University Press, 1952.

_____. *The Structure of Social Action*. New York: McGraw-Hill Book Company, 1937.

Roethlisberger, F.J. and W.J. Dickson. *Management and the Worker*. Cambridge, Massachusetts: Harvard University Press, 1943.

Rommetveit, Ragnor. *Social Norms and Roles*. Minneapolis, Minnesota: University of Minnesota Press, 1955.

Rourke, Francis E. and Glenn E. Brooks. *The Management Revolution in Higher Education*. Baltimore, Maryland: The John Hopkins Press, 1966.

Selznick, Philip. *TVA and the Grass Roots: A Study in the Sociology of Formal Organization*. Los Angeles: University of California Press, 1953.

Shaw, Clifford. *Brothers in Crime*. Chicago: University of Chicago Press, 1938.

Sheriakov, G.V. and F. Redl. *Discipline for Today's Children and Youth*. Washington, D.C.: Association for Supervision and Curriculum Development, 1944.

Sherif, Muzafer. *The Psychology of Social Norms*. New York: Harper and Brothers Publishers, 1936.

Shih, K. *China Enters the Machine Age*. Cambridge, Massachusetts: Harvard University Press, 1944.

Sills, D.L. *The Volunteers: Means and Ends in a National Organization*. New York: Columbia University Press, 1957.

Simpson, R.F. *Problems of Education Planning in Hong Kong*. Hong Kong: Hong Kong Council of Education Research, 1966.

Sorokin, Pitirim A. *Society, Culture, and Personality*. New York: The Free Press, 1951.

Stouffer, S.A. *et al. The American Soldier*. Princeton, New Jersey: Princeton University Press, 1949.

Stroup, Herbert. *Bureaucracy in Higher Education*. New York: The Free Press, 1966.

Thibaut, John W., and Harold H. Kelley. *The Social Psychology of Groups*. New York: John Wiley and Sons, Inc., 1959.

Thomas, W.I. *On Social Organization and Social Personality*. Chicago: University of Chicago Press, 1966.

_____, and Florian Znaniecki. *The Polish Peasant in Europe and America*. New York: Dover Publications, 1958.

Thompson, J.D., P.B. Hammond, R.W. Hawker, B.H. Junker and A. Tuden (eds.). *Comparative Studies in Administration*. Pittsburg: University of Pittsburg, 1959.

Thrasher, Frederick. *The Gang*. Chicago: The University of Chicago Press, 1927.

Tonnies, Ferdinand. *Community and Society: Gemeinschaft and Gesellschaft*. Edited and translated by Charles P. Loomis. New York: Harper Torchbook, 1957.

Vidich, Arthur J., and Joseph Bensman. *Small Town in Mass Society.* Princeton, New Jersey: Princeton University Press, 1958.

Waley, A. *The Opium War Through Chinese Eyes.* London: Allen and Unwin, 1958.

Warner, W. Lloyd. *Yankee City.* New Haven: Yale University Press, 1963.

Weber, Max. *Economy and Society.* Gunther Roth and Claus Wittich, editors. New York: Bedminster Press, 1968.

Weiss, R.S. *Processes in Organization.* Ann Arbor, Michigan: Survey Research Center, University of Michigan, 1956.

Whisson, Michael G. *Under the Rug.* Hong Kong: The South China Morning Post, Ltd., 1965.

Whyte, William. *Street Corner Society.* Chicago: University of Chicago Press, 1955.

Williams, Robert L. *The Administration of Academic Affairs in Higher Education.* Ann Arbor, Michigan: The University of Michigan Press, 1965.

Willaims, Robin M., Jr. *American Society.* Third edition. New York: Alfred A. Knopf, 1960.

B. JOURNALS AND ARTICLES

Aiken, Michael, and Gerald Hoge. "Organizational Alienation: A Comparative Analysis," *American Sociological Review,* 31:497-507, August, 1966.

Bates, Frederick L. "A Conceptual Analysis of Group Structure," *Social Forces,* 35:103-11, No. 3, 1957.

_____, and H.L. Nix. "Social Disorganization of the Group Level: A Role Theory Approach," *United College Journal.* Hong Kong, Vol. 3, 1964.

_____. "Position, Role, and Status: A Reformulation of Concepts," *Social Forces,* 34: 313-21, No. 4, May, 1956.

_____. "Institutions, Organizations, and Communities," *The Pacific Sociological Review,* Vol. 3, No. 2, 1960.

Becker, Howard. "Constructive Typology in the Social Sciences," *American Sociological Review,* Vol. V, No. 1, February, 1940.

Bendix, R. "Bureaucracy, The Problem and Its Setting," *American Sociological Review,* 12:493-507, 1947.

Bertrand, Alvin L. "Stress-Strain Elements of Social Systems: A Micro Theory of Conflict and Change," *Social Forces,* 42:1-9, October, 1963.

_____. "A Structural Analysis of Differential Patterns of Social Relations, A Role Theory Perspective for Rural Sociology," A Presidential address delivered at the 1968 annual meeting of the Rural Sociology Society, Boston, Massachusetts, August, 1968.

Bierstedt, R. "An Analysis of Social Power," *American Sociological Review*, 15:730-38, 1950.

Blau, P.M. "Cooperation and Competition in a Bureaucracy," *American Journal of Sociology*, 59:530-35, 1954.

_____. "Formal Organization: Dimension of Analysis," *American Journal of Sociology*, 63:58-69, July, 1957.

_____. "Structural Effects," *American Sociological Review*, 25:178-93, 1960.

_____, Wolf V. Heydebrand, and Robert E. Stauffer. "The Structure of Small Bureaucracies," *American Sociological Review*, 31:179-91, April, 1966.

Borgatta, E.F., R.F. Bales, and A.S. Couch. "Some Findings Relevant to the Great Man Theory of Leadership," *American Sociological Review*, 19:755-59, 1954.

Caplow, T. "The Criteria of Organizational Success," *Social Forces*, 32:1-9, 1953.

Cicourel, A.V. "The Front and Back of Organizational Leadership, A Case Study," *The Pacific Sociological Review*, 1:54-58, 1948.

Clark, Peter B., and J.Q. Wilson. "Incentive Systems: A Theory of Organizations," *Administrative Science Quarterly*, 6:129-66, September, 1961.

Coates, C.H., and R.J. Pellegrin. "Executives and Supervisors," *American Sociological Review*, 22:217-22, 1957.

Coleman, J.S. "The Adolescent Subculture and Academic Achievement," *American Journal of Sociology*, 65:337-47, 1960.

Constas, Helen. "Max Weber's Two Conceptions of Bureaucracy," *American Journal of Sociology*, 63:400-409, 1958.

Davis, A.K. "Bureaucratic Patterns in the Navy Officers' Corps," Robert K. Merton, *et al. Reader in Bureaucracy*. New York: The Free Press, 1952.

Davis, James A., Joe E. Spaeth, and Carolyn Huson. "A Technique for Analyzing the Effects of Group Composition," *American Sociological Review*, 26:215-25, 1961.

Davis, Kingsley. "The Myth of Functional Analysis as a Special Method in Sociology and Anthropology," *American Sociological Review*, 24:757-72, December, 1959.

Duncan, Otis Dudley. "Cultural, Behavioral, and Ecological Perspectives in the Study of Social Organization," *American Journal of Sociology*, 65:132-46, September, 1959.

Eisenstadt, S.N. "Bureaucracy and Bureaucratization," *Current Sociology*, 7:99-124, 1958.

Etzioni, Amatai. "Critical Look at System Model," *Administrative Science Quarterly*, 5:259-78, September, 1960.

_____. "The Functional Differentiation of Elites in the Kibbutz," *American Journal of Sociology*, 64:476-87, 1959.

Etzioni, Amatai. "Two Approaches to Organizational Effectiveness: A Critique and a Suggestion," *Administrative Science Quarterly*, 5:257-78, 1960.

Frank, A.G. "Goal Ambiguity and Conflicting Standards: An Approach to the Study of Organization," *Human Organization*, 17:8-13, 1957-58.

Georgepoulos, B.S., and A.S. Tannembaum. "A Study of Organizational Effectiveness," *American Sociological Review*, 22:534-40, 1957.

Gross, Edward. "Some Functional Consequences of Primary Controls in Formal Work Organizations," *American Sociological Review,* 18:368-73, August, 1953.

Grusky, Oscar. "Administrative Succession in Formal Organization," *Social Forces,* 39:105-15, 1960.

Guetzkow, H., and W.R. Dill. "Factors in Organizational Development of Task-oriented Groups," *Sociometry,* 20:175-204, 1959.

Gusfield, Joseph R. "Social Structure and Moral Reform: A Study of the Women's Christian Temperance Union," *American Journal of Sociology,* 61:221-32, 1955.

Gyr, J. "Analysis of Committee Member Behavior in Four Cultures," *Human Relations,* 4:193-202, 1951.

Hagen, Everett E. "Analytical Models in the Study of Social System," *American Journal of Sociology,* pp. 144-51, September, 1961.

Hawley, Amos H., Walter Boland, and Margaret Boland. "Population Size and Administration in Institutions of Higher Learning," *American Sociological Review,* 30:252-55, April, 1965.

Homans, George C. "Bringing Men Back In," *American Sociological Review,* 29:809-18, December, 1969.

Julian, Joseph, "Compliance Patterns and Communication Blocks in Complex Organizations," *American Sociological Review,* 31:282-89, June, 1966.

Karsh, B., J. Suchman, and Daisy M. Lilienthal. "The Union Organizer and His Tactics: A Case Study," *American Journal of Sociology,* 59:113-22, 1953.

Katz, E., and S.N. Eisenstadt. "Some Sociological Observations on the Response of Israeli Organizations to New Immigration," *Administrative Science Quarterly,* 5:111-33, 1960.

Lefton, Mark and William R. Rosengren. "Organizations and Clients: Lateral and Longitudinal Dimensions," *American Sociological Review,* 31:802-10, December, 1966.

Marcus, P.M. "Expressive and Instrumental Groups," *American Sociological Review,* 66:54-59, 1960.

Mulligan, Raymond A. "Social Characteristics of College Students," *American Sociological Review,* 18:305-10, 1953.

———. "Socioeconomic Background and College Enrollment," *American Sociological Review,* 16:188-96, 1951.

Nix, Harold L., and Frederick L. Bates. "Occupational Role Stress: A Structural Approach," *Rural Sociology,* Vol. 27, No. 1, March, 1962.

Olive, Betsy Ann. "The Administration of Higher Education," *Administrative Science Quarterly,* II:671-77, 1966-67.

Parsons, Talcott. "Suggestions for a Sociological Approach to the Theory of Organization," *Administrative Science Quarterly,* 1:63-85, June, 1956.

Phelan, J. L. "Authority and Flexibility in the Spanish Imperial Bureaucracy," *Administrative Science Quarterly,* 5:47-65, 1960.

Presthus, R.V. "Bureaucracy and Behavior in Many Cultures," *Public Administrative Review,* 19:25-35, 1959.

———. "Social Bases of Bureaucratic Organization," *Social Forces,* 38:103-109, 1959.

Reissman, L. "A Study in Role Conceptions in Bureaucracy," *Social Forces,* 27:305-10, 1949.

Rettig, S.S., F.N. Jacobson and B. Pasamanick. "Status Overestimation, Objective Status, and Job Satisfaction among Professors," *American Sociological Review*, 23:75-81, 1958.

Sanford, Nevitt. "Personality Development During the College Years," *The Journal of Social Issues*, 12:1-70, No. 4, 1956.

Schwartz, Norris S., and Charlotte G. Schwartz. "Problems in Participant Observation," *American Journal of Sociology*, 60:350-51, January, 1955.

Scudder, K.J. "The Open Institution," *Annals of the American Academy of Political Social Science*, 293:80-82, 1954.

Seeman, M., and R.T. Morris. "The Problem of Leadership: An Interdisciplinary Approach," *Social Forces*, 56:149-55, 1950.

Selznick, P. "Foundations of the Theory of Organization," *American Sociological Review*, 13:25-35, 1948.

Shor, E.L. "The Thai Bureaucracy," *Administrative Science Quarterly*, 5:66-86, 1960.

Simmel, G. "Superiority and Subordination as Subject Matter in Sociology," *American Journal of Sociology*, 2:167-89, 1896.

Alater, P.E. "Role Eifferences in Small Groups," *American Sociological Review*, 20:300-10, 1959.

Tannenbaum, S., and Gerald G. Bachman. "Structural Versus Individual Effects," *American Journal of Sociology*, 69:585-97, May, 1964.

Thomas, E.J. "Role Conceptions and Organization Size," *American Sociological Review*, 24:30-37, 1959.

Thompson, J.D., and M.J. McEwen. "Organizational Goals and Environment," *American Sociological Review*, 23:23-31, 1958.

_____. "Organizational Management and Conflict," *Administrative Science Quarterly*, 4: 389-409, 1960.

Udy, S.H., Jr. "The Structure of Authority in Non-industrial Production Organizations," *American Journal of Sociology*, 64:582-84, 1959.

_____. " 'Bureaucracy' and 'Rationality' Weber's Organizational Theory: An Empirical Study," *American Sociological Review*, 24:791-95, 1959.

Wilson, Logan. "Academic Administration: Its Abuses and Uses," *American Association of University Professors*, 41:684-92, Winter, 1955.

Worthy, James C. "Organizational Structure and Employee Morale," *American Sociological Review*, 15:169-79, April, 1950.

C. ESSAYS

Angell, R.C., and R. Freedman. "The Use of Documents, Records, and Census Materials and Indices," *Research Methods in the Behavioral Sciences*, L. Festinger and D. Katz, editors. New York: Dryden Press, 1953, Pp. 300-26.

Bates, Frederick L. *An Outline of Structural Concepts.* Mimeographed. Baton Rouge, Louisiana: Department of Sociology, Louisiana State University, December, 1968.

Bidwell, Charles E. "The School as A Formal Organization," *Handbook of Organizations,* James G. March, editor. Chicago: Rand McNally and Company, 1965.

Buckley, Walter. "Structural-Functional Analysis in Modern Sociology," *Modern Sociological Theory in Continuity and Change,* Howard Becker and Alvin Boskoff, editors. New York: Holt, Rinehart, and Winston, 1957. Pp. 236-59.

Goffman, E. "The Characteristics of Total Institutions," *Symposium on Preventive and Social Psychiatry.* Washington, D.C.: Walter Reed Army Institute of Research, 1957. Pp. 43-84.

Gross, Neal. "The Sociology of Education," *Sociology Today,* Robert K. Merton, Leonard Broom, Leonard S. Cottrell, Jr., editors. New York: Basic Books, 1959. Chapter V.

Martindale, Don. "Limits of and Alternatives to Functionalism in Sociology," *Functionalism in the Social Sciences.* Philadelphia: The American Academy of Political and Social Sciences, February, 1965. Pp. 156-60.

Scott, W. Richard. "Field Methods in the Study of Organization," *Handbook of Organizations,* James G. March, editor. Chicago: Rand McNally and Company, 1965. Pp. 286-87.

D. RECORDS, MINUTES, YEARBOOKS, AND CENSUS MATERIAL

Hong Kong Baptist Association Meeting Minutes and Office Records, 1955-69.

Hong Kong Baptist College Academic Committee and Board Meetings, 1959-69.

Hong Kong Baptist College Accountant's Office Records, 1956-68.

Hong Kong Baptist College Annual Bulletins, 1957-68.

Hong Kong Baptist College Board of Trustees Executive Committee Meeting Minutes, 1956-68.

Hong Kong Baptist College Board of Trustees (Governors) Meeting Minutes, 1956-68.

Hong Kong Baptist College Comptroller's Office Records, 1963-68.

Hong Kong Baptist College Dean of Students Office Records, 1956-68.

Hong Kong Baptist College Dean of Studies' Office Records, 1956-69.

Hong Kong Baptist College Faculty and Staff Meeting Minutes, 1956-68.

Hong Kong Baptist College Registrar's Office Records, 1956-68.

Hong Kong Baptist College Religious Director's Office Records, 1956-68.

Hong Kong Baptist College Statement of Accounts, 1956-68, Lowe, Bigham, and Matthews, chartered accountants.

Hong Kong Baptist College Vice President's Personal Correspondence, 1958-59, 1964-65, 1968-69.

Hong Kong Baptist College Vice President's Official Correspondence, 1956-69.

Hong Kong Baptist College Yearbooks, 1960-68.

The Hong Kong Census, 1961. Hong Kong: Government Printing Press, 1962.

Hong Kong Macau Baptist Mission Meetings, 1954-69.

The Hong Kong Report, 1957. Hong Kong: Hong Kong Government Press, 1958.

The Hong Kong Report, 1968. Hong Kong: Hong Kong Government Press, 1969.

Appendix

Appendix

APPENDIX A

ORIGINAL CONSTITUTION
HONG KONG BAPTIST COLLEGE

ARTICLE I — Name

The Name of this institution shall be the Hong Kong Baptist College.

ARTICLE II — Location

The College shall be located in Hong Kong.

ARTICLE III — Purpose

This institution shall provide higher education for Middle School graduates, both men and women, in an environment which is thoroughly Christian, so that each student may be well-grounded in the Christian philosophy of life. It shall maintain a high academic standard and provide moral and spiritual training so that the student may be equipped for a useful life as a leader in the modern world.

In seeking to achieve the above purposes the school shall endeavor to maintain an atmosphere of scientific enquiry in the search for truth in all areas of human achievement. Furthermore, it shall strive to achieve these purposes and conduct its program in accordance with the great historic principles of the Baptist faith.

ARTICLE IV — Board of Trustees

Section 1. Relationship to the College. The Board of Trustees shall elect a president and vice-president of the college. It shall be responsible for the granting of all degrees and diplomas to approved candidates. The Board of Trustees shall be responsible to The United H.K. Christian Baptist Churches Association (1) for setting up the school's general policies and principles and seeing that they are carried out by the administrative officials, (2) for the use, oversight and up-keep of all college property, (3) for general policy as to budget and general expenditure of the college, and (4) for approving the courses of study, faculty and other administrative officers.

Section 2. The Executive Committee of The United H.K. Christian Baptist Churches Association shall choose a committee prior to the Annual Meeting of the Association to nominate members of the Board of Trustees according to the following plan:

(1) If available nine members shall be chosen from the Board of Trustees of Pui Ching and Pooi To Middle Schools; if available nine members shall be chosen from the Hong Kong-Macau Mission of the Foreign Mission Board of the Southern Baptist Convention; and nine (or more if necessary to make up the total of twenty-seven) members shall be chosen from members of cooperating churches of The United H.K. Christian Baptist Churches Association.

(2) The twenty-seven members shall be divided into three groups of nine members, each of which shall serve terms of three years duration, but it shall be arranged in such a way that one group of nine shall be elected annually for three years terms of service. Thus, The United H.K. Christian Baptist Churches Association in Annual Meeting will elect one-third of the Board members annually according to this plan of rotation.

Any trustee shall be eligible for re-election.

Section 3. A majority of the members shall constitute a quorum for the transaction of business.

Section 4. The President and the Vice-President of the college are members of the Board by virtue of office but without vote. Other administration officers of Faculty members who receive salaries for more than half-time services are not eligible for membership on the Board.

Section 5. For any cause deemed sufficient to the members of the Board a member may be retired from the Board by a vote of not less than (19) nineteen members, subject, however, to appeal to The United H.K. Christian Baptist Churches Association.

Section 6. If deemed wise by the Board of Trustees any vacancy may be temporarily filled by majority vote of the Board, such person to serve until the annual meeting of the Association. In any case the Association should be notified immediately of any action taken.

Section 7. There shall be regular Quarterly meetings of the Board, that is four each year. Each member of the Board shall be sent a written notice of the time and place of meeting at least one week prior to the meeting.

Section 8. Special meetings may be called by the Chairman of the Board of Trustees on a written request of either the President or the Vice-President of the college, or by the Executive Committee or by (9) nine members of the Board of Trustees. The Chairman of the Board of Trustees, may at any time in his own discretion call a special meeting. The Executive Committee, or nine petitioning members of the Board of Trustees, may call a special meeting of the Board. Only business necessitating the meeting may be attended to at a special session of the Board. Advance notice of special meetings shall be given in writing to each board member one week prior to meetings.

Section 9. The meetings of the Board shall be conducted according to the usual rules of parlimentary law.

ARTICLE V — Officers of the Board of Trustees

Section 1. The officers of the Board of Trustees shall be a Chairman, a Vice-Chairman, a Secretary, and a Treasurer. Each of these officers shall be elected at the Spring Meeting of the Board for the term of one year.

Section 2. (1) The *Chairman* of the Board shall preside at the meetings of the Board, preserve proper decorum, decide all questions of order, subject to appeal to the Board, and appoint all committees unless otherwise ordered. He shall sign with the Secretary diplomas, orders, and any and all acts of the Board requiring authentication.

(2) In the absence of the Chairman, or in event of his disability, the *Vice-Chairman* shall act in his stead.

(3) The *Secretary* shall keep the minutes of the transaction of the Board, enrolling the names of the members present, preserve for ready reference all acts, rules and regulations of the Board, keep on file all documents, reports and papers belonging to the Board, and perform all the duties and correspondence usually appertaining to this office not otherwise provided for.

(4) The *Treasurer* shall have oversight of all funds of the college and their disbursement, and he shall make to the Board annually or at such other times as may be specified, a statement of the receipts and disbursements and a detailed report of the condition of each separate fund.

ARTICLE VI — Executive Committee

Section 1. There shall be an Executive Committee of nine members to be elected annually at the Spring Meeting.

Section 2. Any action passed by this Committee shall have the approval of at least five members, that is, majority of the committee of nine.

Section 3. This Committee shall have power between the meetings of the Board of Trustees to perform all duties necessary to the operation of the Col-

Board of Trustees to perform all duties necessary to the operation of the College. All actions of the Executive Committee shall be reported to the Board of Trustees at regular meetings for approval.

Section 4. The officers of the Board shall be officers of the Executive Committee. The Chairman shall perform the usual duties. The Secretary shall keep a permanent record of the proceedings of the meetings and report to the Board.

Section 5. The meetings of the Executive Committee shall be held at the call of the Chairman or Vice-Chairman of the Board or by written petition by a majority of the members of the Committee.

ARTICLE VII — Officers of Administration

Section 1. The officers of administration shall consist of the President, Vice-President, Dean of Studies, and such other officers and persons as may be necessary to carry on the affairs of the institution. The President and the Vice-President shall be elected by the Board of Trustees for any period specified by the Board. All other officers and persons of the Administration shall be elected by the Board of Trustees upon nomination or recommendation by the President of the College.

Section 2. The President shall be the responsible head of this institution. He shall be responsible to the Board of Trustees for any and all acts or matters relating to the administrative life and progress of the institution. He shall represent the college in all legal and business matters in and out of court, and with the government. He shall sign and confer all diplomas and degrees.

Section 3. The Vice-President shall administer the affairs of the College when the President is away from the Colony or in case of his incapacity for any reason. He shall at all times work in close cooperation with the President.

Section 4. The Dean or Deans and other administrative officers shall perform such duties as may be outlined by the President and approved by the Board of Trustees.

ARTICLE VIII — Religious Affiliation of Administrative and Teaching Staff

All administrative officials shall be active members of one of the Hong Kong Baptist churches. At least three-fourths of the faculty and staff members must be Christians, and, among them, a majority shall be Baptists.

ARTICLE IX — Property and Finance

Section 1. All property of the College, whether it be land, buildings, or moveable equipment, shall be held in the name of The United H.K. Christian Baptist Churches Association. The Board of Trustees shall be entrusted with their use, oversight, and up-keep.

Section 2. All money for operating expenses of the College, whether gifts, tuition, or collections from any source, shall be kept in a Bank agreed upon by the Board of Trustees in the name of the college. A record shall be kept of all monies received and disbursed, and monthly reports shall be made by the college administration to the Board of Trustees. Money can be drawn only according to the budget approved by the Board of Trustees. The signature of one official of the college chosen by the Board of Trustees shall appear on all checks. In addition, one of four college officials or Trustee members chosen by the Board of Trustees shall countersign all checks. The Bursar of the college shall be bonded to the amount set by the Board of Trustees. An annual audit shall be made by the Board of Trustees of the college each year by a certified auditor.

ARTICLE X — Committees

The Board of Trustees may set up committees, in addition to the Executive Committee, either of a permanent or temporary nature, as it deems wise in the fulfilment of its duties.

ARTICLE XI — Effective Date

This constitution shall go into effect at the time it is approved by majority vote in the Annual Meeting of The United H.K. Christian Baptist Churches Association.

ARTICLE XII — Amendments

Any proposed amendment must be presented in writing to the Board of Trustees at one of the Quarterly-Meetings. The proposed amendment will be acted upon at the following Quarterly-Meeting. It must be approved by at least nineteen members of the Board of Trustees. It become effective after presentation to and approval by the United H.K. Christian Baptist Churches Association in Annual Meeting.

SALARIES BASED ON ACADEMIC QUALIFICATIONS AND SPECIAL FACTORS AS OF JUNE, 1967 (WOMEN AT 90 PERCENT OF SCALE) THROUGH ASSISTANT LECTURER LEVEL

1. Administration

Dean of Students
Religious Director
Deans of Faculties
Comptroller
Dean of Studies

1.	Ph.D.'s	$2,200.00	+	(90 X 10)	$900.00	=	$3,100.00
2.	M.A.'s	2,000.00	+	(90 X 10)	900.00	=	2,900.00
3.	All Others	1,800.00	+	(90 X 10)	900.00	=	2,700.00

2. Senior Lecturers

1. Ph.D.'s $2,400.00   +   (90 X 5) $450.00   = $2,850.00
(Minimum of 5 years full-time college teaching after conferring of degree)

2. M.A.'s $2,250.00   +   (80 X 5) $400.00   = $2,450.00
(Minimum of 15 years of full-time college teaching in field of specialization, or equivalent in distinguished research, writing or relevant experience)

3. B.A.'s $1,850.00   +   (70 X 5) $350.00   = $2,200.00
                    (Minimum of 18 years of full-time college teaching after
                    receiving degree, or distinguished research, writing or
                    teaching ability. Only rarely will a person be advanced to
                    this level)

3. Lecturers

1. Ph.D.'s $2,000.00   +   (80 X 4) $320.00   = $2,320.00
                    (Previous teaching experience after conferring of degree
                    not required but desirable to start at this level)

2. M.A.'s $1,700.00   +   (60 X 8) $480.00   = $2,180.00
                    (Minimum of 6 years of full-time college teaching after
                    receiving degree before promotion to this position or all
                    requirements met for Ph.D. except dissertation. In cer-
                    tain cases, distinguished teaching in field or relevant ex-
                    perience prior to degree will count)

3. B.A.'s $1,400.00   +   (50 X 8) $400.00   = $1,800.00
                    (Must have had 2 years or more of graduate study be-
                    yond B.A. degree plus nine year of College teaching ex-
                    perience, or a minimum of 12 years of college teaching;
                    or distinction in writing or teaching ability)

4. Assistant Lecturers

1. M.A. $1,400.00   +   (50 X 5) $250.00   = $1,650.00
                    (Previous teaching experience after conferring of Univer-
                    sity degree desirable but not required to start at this
                    level. A person beginning at any point in (2) may rise by
                    annual increment into this rank)

2. $1,200.00   +   (40 X 4) $160.00   = $1,360.00
                    (Must have completed courses requirements for Universi-
                    ty Master's degree or equivalent (B.A. Honours) or 4
                    years college teaching as tutor or 10 years teaching ex-
                    perience in field, at least four of which are college level)

5. Tutor/Demonstrator *(Rates of pay are the same for men and women)*

   1. **B.A.**   Plus one year of graduate study or 9 years teaching experience in field or other experience providing maturity or skill.

                $1,050.00   +   (40 X 3) $120.00   = $1,170.00

   2. **B.A.**   Or equivalent plus 6 years full-time teaching or other experience related to field or 6 years assistantship.

                $900.00   +   (35 X 3) $105.00   = $1,005.00

6. Assistant *(Rates of pay are the same for men and women)*

   1. **B.A.**   Or equivalent. No experience required to start at this level.

                $600.00   +   (35 X 5) $175.00   = $775.00

7. Senior Clerk, Senior Typist *(Clerical and other non-teaching staff)*

                $450.00   +   (30 X 10) $300.00   = $750.00
(College diploma or B.A. degree or specialization and experience for position)

8. Junior Clerk, Junior Typist *(Clerical and other non-teaching staff)*

                $300.00   +   (25 X 5) $125.00   = $425.00
(Middle school diploma or specialization and experience so as to function efficiently in position)

9. Servants and Other Staff *(Driver, watchmen, etc.)*

       (Pay on monthly basis according to prevailing rates)

Notes

1. Movement from lower to higher rank is not automatic but dependent on recommendation of responsible superiors plus administrative approval and Board action.

2. Department Heads get $100.00 per month additional to scale. This includes the Librarian Acting Department Heads and Assistant Department Heads get $75.00 per month additional to scale. This also includes the Secretary to the President, the Assistant Dean of Studies, the Registrar, the Business Manager and the Accountant.
3. Deans of Faculties teach up to 3 courses, up to 10 semester hours or equivalent per week.
   Department Heads and Lecturers with special responsibility teach 4 courses, up to 12 semester hours per week.
4. Full-time lecturers teach up to 15 semester hours or equivalent per week.

APPENDIX C

REVISED CONSTITUTION
HONG KONG BAPTIST COLLEGE

1.   The Hong Kong Baptist College was founded in   **Foundation.**
1956 by the United Hong Kong Christian Baptist Churches
Association to provide Christian Higher Education.

2.   In this Constitution, unless the context other-   **Interpretation.**
wise requires —

"Association" means the United Hong Kong Christian Bap-
    tist Churches Association;

"Board," "Council" and "Academic Board" respectively
    mean the Board of Governors, Council and Academic
    Board of the College;

"College" means the Hong Kong Baptist College;

"Constitution" means the constitution of the College;

"Director" means the Director of Education;

"President," "Vice-President," "Dean of Studies," "Dean
    of Students," "Chaplain" and "Comptroller" respec-
    tively mean the President, Vice-President, Dean of
    Studies, Dean of Students, Chaplain and Comptroller
    of the College.

3.   The College shall be located in Hong Kong.   **Location.**

4.   The administration of the College shall be   **Administration.**
vested in:

(a)   The Board of Governors;

(b)   The College Council;

(c)   The Academic Board;

(d)   The Boards of Faculties;

or any Committees appointed by the foregoing under the provisions of this Constitution together with the officers of the College.

5.   (1)   The Board shall be constituted as follows: **Board of**

(i)   18 persons to be elected in the following   **Governors.**
manner:

(a)   Subject to the adoption of this Constitution by a special general meeting of the Association, held more than one month before the annual general meeting of the Association, the Executive Board of the Association shall nominate in writing 18 members of the Association for election to the Board of the College. Such nominations shall be made at least one month before the annual general meeting. In addition to those nominations, individual members of the Association may nominate and second other members of the Association or persons recognized as members of co-operating Baptist Churches of Hong Kong by the Executive Board of the Association. Such nominations shall be in writing and shall contain the full names, addresses and signatures of the nominee, proposer and seconder and shall indicate whether the nominee is a member of the Association and shall be forwarded to the Executive Board of the Association at least fourteen days before the annual general meeting of the Association.

(b)   At the annual general meeting of Association, members of the Association present shall elect, by secret ballot, 18 members of the Board from the above nominees. The 18 members so elected shall be divided into three groups of six according to the number of votes polled by them. The first group shall consist of the six members elected who have polled the greatest number of votes who shall hold office for three years. The second group shall consist of the six members elected who have polled the next greatest

number of votes who shall hold office for two years. The third group shall consist of the remainder of the eighteen members elected who shall hold office for one year. In the case of equality of votes a ballot shall decide in which group the persons with equality of votes shall serve.

(c) After the first election, in each year six members shall be elected to replace the six members whose term of office has expired. The provisions of the preceding subparagraph *(a)* and *(b)* shall apply to the election of the six members to be elected with the necessary modification as to the number of members to be elected but the members of the Board elected pursuant to his sub-clause shall hold office for three years.

(d) Any member of the Board elected in accordance with the above provisions shall be eligible to stand for reelection.

(ii) The members of the Board elected in accordance with Section 4 (i) may, subject to the subsequent endorsement of the Executive Board of the Association, appoint up to six additonal members of the Board, who may or may not be members of the Association, for a team of one year. Persons so appointed shall not be eligible for reappointment for more than three successive terms.

(2) The Board shall, form among its elected members, appoint a Chairman, Vice-Chairman, Honorary Treasurer and Honorary Secretary, who shall hold office for one year from date of appointment or until such member ceases to be a member of the Board whichever shall first happen. Retiring office holder shall be eligible for reappointment. Elections for such appointments shall be held at the first Board meeting after the election of members of the Board in any year.

(3) Vacancies shall be filled as they occur or as soon afterwards as conveniently possible.

(4) Any member of the Board wishing to re-

sign shall do so by written request addressed to the Honorable Secretary.

(5)   If any elected member of the Board dies, or remains out of the Colony for more than three months without the permission of the Board, or gives notice of his intended absence for more than three months, or desires to be discharged from his duties as a member of the Board or refuses or is unfit to act or is incapable of acting as a member of the Board, the Association may elect another person who is eligible for election to act as a member of the Board in his place. The member of the Board so elected shall hold office until the expiration of the term of office of the member of the Board so replaced.

6.   The Board shall:

(1)   Be the supreme Governing Body of the College and be responsible for the general direction of the College, its property, functions and affairs, and have the power to revoke any decision of the College Council, the Academic Board or the Board of any Faculty, or any committee appointed by such bodies.

Functions of Board of Governors.

(2)   Direct the development of the College and procure legislation.

(3)   Control the finances of the College and have power to determine finally any question of finance arising out of administration of the College or the execution of its policy or in the execution of any trust requiring execution by the College, provided that, before determining any question of finances which directly affects the educational policy of the College, it shall invite the opinion of the Academic Board and take into consideration any recommendation or report made by such board or by the President.

(4)   Be responsible for all measures necessary or desirable for the conservation or augmentation of the resources of the College, and for this purpose may from time to time specify any matter affecting the income or expenditure of the College in respect of which the consent

of the Board shall be obtained before action is taken or liability incurred.

(5)   Receive and consider an annual report from the College Council not later than 31st October each year and such special reports as the Council may decide to submit, and to pass such resolutions or make such directives thereon as it may think fit.

(6)   Receive for approval an annual statement from the Comptroller of the estimated expenditure and revenue of the College for the ensuing financial year.

(7)   Receive from the Honorary Treasurer the Annual audited accounts of the College which he has received from the Comptroller - and pass such resolutions or make such directives thereon as it may think fit.

(8)   Appoint or terminate the appointment of the President of the College on the advice of the College Council and Determine the conditions of service of the President, which said conditions shall be embodied in a written contract, but any such appointment or termination shall be subject to the approval of the Director of Education.

(9)   Appoint or terminate the appointment of the Vice-President of the College and determine the conditions of service. Such conditions shall be embodied in a written contract.

(10)   Shall elect or terminate the appointment of the Chairman, Vice-Chairman, Honorable Treasurer and Honorable Secretary of the Board.

(11)   At its discretion accept, on behalf of the College, by way of gift, testamentary disposition or otherwise, property and moneys in aid of the finances or aims and objects of the College on such conditions (not inconsistent with the provisions of the Ordinance incorporating the College) as it may determine.

7.   (1)   The Board shall hold regular meetings at least twice in each academic year.

(2)   One week's notice shall be given for each regular meeting.

(3)   The Chairman of the Board may convene

Meetings of the Board of Governors.

a special meeting of the Board at any time and shall do so on the written request of a minimum of five members.

(4)   Every question arising at any meeting of the Board shall be decided by a majority of votes of the members present and voting thereon each such person having not more than one vote thereon.

(5)   One half of the members of the Board for the time being shall constitute a quorum.

(6)   The Chairman of the Board may require any officer or teacher to be present at any meeting of the Board to assist or give information.

(7)   If a member has any pecuniary interest, direct or indirect, in any written contract or proposed ocntract or other matter, and is present at a meeting of the Board at which the written contract or other matter is the subject of consideration, he shall as soon as practicable after the commencement of the meeting, disclose to the Board the fact and nature of his interest, and the Board may require him to leave the meeting whilst the matter is being dealt with.

8.   (1)   The College Council shall consist of: **The College**

(i)   The following officers of the Board ex-officio: **Council.**
The Chairman of the Board who shall be chairman;
The Vice-Chairman of the Board who shall be Vice-Chairman;
The Honorary Treasurer;
The Honorary Secretary.

(ii)   Three additional elected members from the Board.

(iii)   The following officers of the College ex-officio:
The President;
The Vice-President;
The Dean of Studies; The Dean of Students; the Chaplain and the Comptroller of the College.

(iv)   In addition the Board may appoint not more than two other persons who are either other officers of the College or full-time teachers of the College.

(2) All members of the College Council shall hold office for one year from the 1st of August, and shall be eligible for re-appointment.

(3) Vacancies shall be filled as they occur, or as soon afterwards as conveniently may be.

(4) Any member of the College Council not being an ex-officio member may resign by written notice addressed to the Secretary of the Council.

(5) If any elected member of the College Council dies, or remains out of the Colony for more than three months without the permission of the Board, or gives notice of his intended absence for more than three months, or desires to be discharged from his duties as a member or refuses or is unfit to act or is incapable of acting as a member, the Board may elect another person to act as a member in his place. The member so elected shall hold office until the expiration of the term of office of the member he replaces.

9. The College Council shall be the executive body of the College administering the property and managing the general affairs of the College subject to the directions of the Board and without prejudice to the generality of such powers shall: **Functions of the College Council.**

(1) supply members of the Board with copies of minutes of all Council meetings and other relevant documents;

(2) under the direction of the Board manage and regulate the accounts, investments, property, business and all affairs whatsoever of the College and for the purpose appoint bankers, auditors, counsel, solicitor and such officers and other agents as it may deem expedient to appoint;

(3) enter into, vary, perform, and cancel contracts on behalf of the College;

(4) prepare, with the adivce of the Finance Committee and any other bodies it may wish to consult,

the annual budget, which shall be submitted to the Board for approval before 1st of June each year in respect of the financial year 1st of August to 31st of July following;

(5)   give directives to the Academic Board or any officer or teacher of the College on any financial matter or any matter affecting the property of the College;

(6)   in consultation with the Academic Board review the instruction and teaching of the College;

(7)   provide for the use of the buildings, libraries, laboratories, premises, furniture, equipment and general facilities required to carry out the work of the College;

(8)   with the exception of the President and Vice-President, Chairman and Vice-Chairman, appoint and dismiss all other officers of the College, subject to the approval of the Board;

(9)   appoint and dismiss teachers as provided by section 27;

(10)   within the framework laid down by the Board approve administration plans, prescribe the duties of officers, teachers, and other employees whom it may appoint and fix their remuneration and the terms and conditions of their appointments and embody such terms and conditions in contract;

(11)   entertain and adjudicate upon complaints from and redress grievances of members of the College and persons employed therein;

(12)   prescribe fees;

(13)   approve regulations;

(14)   delegate any of its power to any member of the Council or to any committee thereof or to any officer or teacher;

(15)   do all other such acts and things as may be requisite to perform any duty which the Board may delegate to the College Council, or to give effect to the powers conferred on the Council by the Post-Secondary College Ordinance or this Constitution.

10.   (1)   The College Council shall meet not less than four times a year.   **Meetings of the College Council.**

(2)   The Chairman of the College Council may convene a meeting of the Council at any time, and shall do so on the written request of a minimum of five members.

(3)   Every question arising at any meeting of the College Council shall be decided by a majority of votes of the members present and voting thereon, each such person having not more than one vote thereon.

(4)   One half of the members of the College Council for the time being shall form a quorum.

(5)   The Chairman of the College Council may require any officer or teacher to be present at any meeting of the College Council to assist or give information.

(6)   If a member has any pecuniary interest, direct or indirect, in any contract or proposed contract or other matter, and is present at a meeting of the College Council at which the contract or other matter is the subject of consideration, he shall as soon as practicable after the commencement of the meeting disclose the fact and nature of his interest to the College Council and ask to be excused from the meeting, and the College Council may require him to leave the meeting whilst the matter is being dealt with.

11.   (1)   The Academic Board shall consist of: **The Academic Board**

The President (who shall be Chairman);

The Vice-President (who shall be Vice-Chairman);

The Dean of Studies;

The Dean of Students;

All Deans of Faculties;

The Senior Lecturers of the College;

All Heads of Teaching Departments, who are not Senior Lecturers;

The Registrar;

The Librarian;

The Chaplain;

and such other persons (not exceeding

two in number) as may be appointed by
the College Council.

(2)   The Registrar of the College shall be the
Secretary of the Academic Board.

12.   The Academic Board shall regulate the academ-   **Functions of the**
ic affairs of the College subject to the financial control of   **Academic Board.**
the College Council, and without prejudice to the generality
of such powers shall:

(i)   in consultation with the Faculty Boards provide
courses of study and tutorials leading to the
diplomas and certificates to be awarded by the
College, and such other courses of study as may
be thought desirable, to direct and regulate the
instruction and education in the College and to
stimulate the advancement of knowledge by research and publications;

(ii)   direct the manner in which College examinations shall be conducted and appoint internal
and external examiners as necessary;

(iii)   decide in accordance with the Constitution and
regulations what persons have qualified for the
award of diplomas, certificates, scholarships,
pri   prizes and other awards or marks of distinction;

(iv)   regulate the admission of students to courses in
the College;

(v)   advise the College Council on the provision of
facilities for educational and other Academic
matters;

(vi)   recommend to the College Council, as necessary, the establishment of additional courses or
teaching posts;

(vii)   recommend to the College Council, on the advice of the President of the College if so desired, any person for appointment to or removal
from the post of teacher;

(viii)   organize the Faculties and review, refer back,
control, amend or disallow any act of the Board
or any Faculty, and give directives to the

Boards of the Faculties;

(ix) manage the libraries, laboratories and museums of the College;

(x) provide for the welfare of and discipline of students;

(xi) expel any student for misconduct or require any student on academic grounds to terminate his studies at the College;

(xii) suspend any student for misconduct, provided that the President may, if he thinks it necessary, in any case peremptorily exercise a like power of suspension pending the decision of the Academic Board in that case;

(xiii) determine the policy to be followed by any hostel maintained by the College, and approve hostels and prescribe the conditions under which students may be permitted to reside therein;

(xiv) approve any lectures and courses of study for persons who are not members of the College;

(xv) draw up any necessary regulations regarding academic affairs, the general well-being and control of students and hostels, for the approval of the Council;

(xvi) give advice on any matter which may be referred to it by the Council;

(xvii) delegate any of its powers to any member of the Academic Board or any Committee thereof or the Board of any Faculty or to any officer or teacher;

(xviii) do all such other matters, acts and things as may be requisite to give effect to the powers conferred on the Academic Board by this Constitution, and by the Post-Secondary College Ordinance Cap. 320 and any other relevant Ordinance.

13. (1) The Academic Board shall meet at least twice in every term in every Academic year.

Meetings of the Academic Board.

(2)   The Chairman of the Academic Board may convene a meeting of the Board at any time and shall do so on the written request of a minimum of five members.

(3)   Every question arising at any meeting of the Academic Board shall be decided by a majority of votes of the members present and voting thereon, each such person having not more than one vote thereon.

(4)   One-half of the members of the Academic Board for the time being shall form a quorum.

(5)   The Chairman of the Academic Board may require any officer or teacher to be present at any meeting of the Board to assist or give information.

(6)   If a member has any pecuniary interest, direct or indirect, in any contract or proposed contract or other matter, and is present at a meeting of the Academic Board at which the contract or other matter is the subject of consideration, he shall as soon as practicable after the commencement of the meeting disclose to the Academic Board the fact and ask to be excused from the meeting, and the Academic Board may require him to leave the meeting whilst the matter is being dealt with.

14.   (1)   There shall be a Faculty Board for each faculty of the College and each Faculty Board shall consist of:

The Faculty Board.

(i)   The Dean of that Faculty, who shall be Chairman;

(ii)   The President;

(iii)   The Vice-President;

(iv)   The Dean of Students;

(v)   The Senior Lecturers, Lecturers and Assistant Lecturers who are members of the Teaching Departments allocated to the Faculty and who are full-time employees of the College.

(vi)   Such other teachers or persons as are appointed by the Academic Board.

(vii)   The Registrar who shall be the Secretary.

(2)   The teachers and persons appointed un-

der paragraph (1) (v) shall hold office for a period of at least one year after the 1st of August in the year of appointment, and shall be eligible for reappointment.

(3)   If for any reason the Dean of the Faculty should be absent from any meeting of the Faculty Board, members of the Faculty Board shall elect from among themselves a person to act as Chairman for the meeting.

15.   Each Faculty Board shall:

Functions of the Faculty Boards.

(i)   be responsible to the Academic Board for the teaching and general organization of the courses assigned to that Faculty reporting thereon from time to time to the Academic Board;

(ii)   advise the Academic Board on any matter relating to the work of that Faculty;

(iii)   do all such other acts and things as may be requisite to perform any duty which the Academic Board may delegate to it.

16.   (1)   Every Faculty Board shall meet at least once in every term in every academic year.

Meetings of the Faculty Boards.

(2)   The Chairman of a Faculty Board may convene a meeting of the Board at any time, and shall do so on the written request of a minimum of three members.

(3)   Every question arising at any meeting of a Faculty Board shall be decided by a majority of votes of the members present and voting thereon, each such person having not more than one vote thereon.

(4)   One-half of the members of a Faculty Board for the time being shall form a quorum.

(5)   The Chairman of a Faculty Board may require any officer or teacher to be present at any meeting of the Board to assist or give information.

(6)   If a member has any pecuniary interest, direct or indirect, in any contract or proposed contract or other matter, and is present at a meeting of the Faculty Board at which the contract or other matter is the subject of consideration, he shall as soon as practicable after the commencement of the meeting, disclose to the Faculty Board the fact and nature of his interest, and the Faculty

Board may require him to leave the meeting whilst the matter is being dealt with.

17.   The Board, College Council, Academic Board and Faculty Boards may establish such committees as they see fit and such committees may be constituted partly of persons who are not members of the particular College body establishing it.   **Committees.**

18.   (1)   The courses given in the College shall be organized for time being under one or more Faculties, as approved by the Academic Board, College Council and Board.   **Teaching Organization.**

(2)   Each Faculty shall have a Dean nominated by the President and appointed by the College Council, subject to control by the Academic Board and the advice of the Board of his Faculty, who shall be in general control of affairs within the Faculty.

(3)   Within each Faculty teachers and courses shall be organized by the Academic Board under Teaching Departments.

(4)   The list of Teaching Departments and their allocation to Faculties shall be prescribed by Regulations made by the Academic Board.

(5)   Every Teaching Department shall have a Chairman nominated by the Dean of the relevant Faculty and approved by the Academic Board.

(6)   The Head of a Teaching Department shall be responsible to the Faculty for the organization of teaching within the Department.

(7)   It shall be permissible for a Teaching Department to be allocated to two or more Faculties.

19.   The following shall be the officers of the College: **Offices.**

(i)   There shall be a President who shall be the Chief academic and administrative Officer of the College.

(ii)   There shall be a Vice-President who shall act for the President on the latter's instructions or whenever the latter is for any reason unable to perform his duties as President.

(iii) There shall be:

    (a)   a Chairman and Vice-Chairman of the Board;

    (b)   a Chairman and Vice-Chairman of the Council;

    (c)   a Chairman and Vice-Chairman of the Academic Board;

    (d)   an Honorary Treasurer of the Board who shall receive from the Comptroller all audited books and shall make annual reports to the Board concerning finances, fund raising, building funds, and related financial matters;

    (e)   an Honorary Secretary of the Board who shall serve also as Honorary Secretary of the College Council, who shall review the minutes of the Board and of the College prepared by the Secretary;

    (f)   a Comptroller;

    (g)   a Chaplain;

    (h)   a Dean of Studies;

    (i)   a Dean of Students;

    (j)   a Dean for each Faculty in the College;

    (k)   a Registrar who shall assist the Dean of Studies;

    (l)   a Librarian who shall assist the Dean of Studies;

    (m)   a Business Manager;

    (n)   an Accountant;

    (o)   such additional officers as may be appointed by the Council subject to the approval of the Board.

(iv) All the officers specified in sub-paragraphs *(f)* to *(l)* of paragraph (iii) shall be appointed and dismissed by the Council subject to the approval of the Board, and their respective terms and conditions of service shall be embodied in a written contract.

20.   It shall be the duty of the President: **Duties of President.**

(i)   to serve as the Administrator of the College, responsible to the Board for all matters pertaining to the student life and progress of the institution;

(ii)   to be responsible for the custody of the College seal and for affixing it to documents pursuant to the directives given by the Board;

(iii)   to see that the provisions of this Constitution and the regulations and all such powers as may be necessary for this purpose are carried out, and, in particular, to ensure that all officers, College bodies, or committees keep within their respective powers;

(iv)   to exercise general supervision over the arrangements for instruction, research, finance, administration, welfare and disciplines in the College, and to report on the above to the Board or the College Council as may be necessary;

(v)   to nominate to the College Council persons for appointment to the posts of Deans of Studies, Dean of Students, Deans of Faculties, Chaplain, Comptroller, and to suggest to the Academic Board persons for appointment to the posts of teachers;

(vi)   to perform such other duties as may be placed upon him by this Constitution and the Regulations or by the Board of Governors.

21.   It shall be the duty of the Vice-President to   **Duties of Vice-President.**
assist the President and to act for the President in his absence, and to perform such other duties as may be placed upon him by this Constitution and the Regulations or by the Board.

22.   The Comptroller shall: **Duties of Comptroller.**

(i)   act as the executive agent of the College in financial and general affairs;

(ii)   be responsible for the keeping of all College accounts and such inventories as the College Council may determine;

(iii)   be responsible for the submission to the auditors of a Balance Sheet and an Income and Expenditure

Account and any other necessary accounts, together with all supporting schedules, as soon as practicable after the end of each financial year;

(iv) be responsible for the general maintenance of all College buildings, properties, and grounds;

(v) keep a register of

(a) Members of the Board;

(b) Members of the College Council;

(vi) perform such other duties as may be determined by the Board and/or College Council.

23.   The Chaplain shall: **Duties of Chaplain.**

(i) act as the executive agent of the College in developing religious life in the College;

(ii) act as religious counsellor to the students;

(iii) promote student and Faculty association and affiliation with Christian churches and institutions;

(iv) perform such other duties as may be determined by the College Council and Academic Board.

24.   The Dean of Studies shall: **Duties of Dean of Studies.**

(i) keep a register of *(a)* all members of the teaching staff, *(b)* members of the Academic Board, *(c)* members of all committees, *(d)* students of the College, *(e)* past students, and *(f)* graduates of the College;

(ii) be responsible for all Academic records and regulations of the College;

(iii) act as the executive agent of the College in academic affairs;

(iv) advise the Academic Board on any questions relating to the work of the Faculties;

(v) perform such other duties as may be determined by the College Council and the Academic Board.

25.   The Dean of Students shall: **Duties of Dean of Students.**

(i) act as the executive agent of the College in developing corporate and social life in the College;

(ii) act as adviser to students;

(iii) be responsible for student discipline;

(iv) be responsible for general health conditions in the College;

(v)   perform such other duties as may be determined by the College Council and Academic Board.

26.   A Dean of Faculty shall be: **Deans of Faculties.**

(i)   The Chairman of the Board of his Faculty, and shall be an ex-officio member of all Committees of such Faculty;

(ii)   an ex-officio member of the Academic Board.

27.   (i)   Teachers shall be classified as senior lec-   **Teachers.** turers, lecturers, assistant lecturers, tutors and demonstrators; and such persons shall be appointed by the College Council on recommendations of the Academic Board subject to the approval of the Board;

(ii)   save from termination at the end of a period of probation the appointment of a teacher may be terminated by the College Council for good cause only, and in every case the College Council shall consider the recommendations of the Academic Board;

(iii)   the minimum qualification of a teacher shall be a university degree;

(iv)   teachers in receipt of full-time salaries from the College shall not engage in outside practice for reward without the consent of the College Council and subject to such conditions as it may impose.

28.   Examinations for College entry, College Diplo-   **Examinations.** mas and College Certificates shall be conducted by examiners appointed by the College Council on the recommendation of the Academic Board.

29.   (i)   In the absence of the Chairman and Vice-   **Procedure** Chairman from a meeting of the Board, College Council,   **Generally.** Academic Board, the Board of any Faculty, or any Committee, the members present shall choose a Chairman to act at the meeting.

(ii)   Except as provided in this Constitution, the Board, College Council, Academic Board, Boards of Faculties and any committees shall determine and make rules for the time and place and procedure of their respective meetings.

(iii)   The minutes of all meetings of every committee

held since the last meeting of the parent body shall be laid on the table at each meeting of that body, whether it will be the Board, the College Council, the Academic Board or the Board of any Faculty.

(iv)   The minutes of all meetings of the Boards of the Faculties held since the last meeting of the Academic Board shall be laid on the table at each meeting of the Academic Board.

(v)   In the case of any equality of votes on a question at any meeting, the Chairman shall have a casting vote.

(vi)   No act or resolution of any College body shall be invalid by reason only of any vacancy in, or any want of qualifications by or validity in the election or appointment of any member of such body.

30.   (i)   The financial year shall be 1st of August to 31st of July.   **Financial Procedure.**

(ii)   The Council shall appoint a Finance Committee, of which the Comptroller shall be secretary and of which the Honorary Treasurer shall be Chairman, to which persons who are not members of the College Council may be appointed.

(iii)   The College Council shall appoint an auditor whose name appears in Part I of the authorized list kept under section 131 of the Companies Ordinance (Cap. 32), who shall sudit the College Accounts annually and shall hold office for one year, but shall be eligible for re-appointment.

(iv)   The Finance Committee shall submit to the Council before 1st of May annually draft estimates of income and expenditure, and such estimates amended as the Council may think fit shall be forwarded to the Board for covering approval before 1st of June annually.

(v)   As soon as practicable after the end of the financial year, a Balance Sheet and Income and Expenditure Account with supporting schedules shall be submitted to the Auditors.

(vi)   The audited accounts, with any comments therein by the Auditors, shall be submitted to the Council and be forwarded by the Council with any comments to the Board.

(vii) The Council may revise the estimates during the course of a financial year, but any such revision which would lead to a deficit or an increased defecit shall not be made without the covering authority of the Board.

(viii) Where property or money is accepted for any special purpose it shall be separately accounted for.

31. (i)   Application for any person to be entered on the register of members of Boards of Governors or of members of College Council shall be made to the Director by the Chairman of the Board on the instructions of the Majority of the same on the prescribed form.

Statutory Provisions for Persons To be Entered on Registers.

(ii)   Application for any person to be entered on the Register of teachers shall be made to the Director by the President subject to the approval of the College Council on the prescribed form.

32. (1)   The College Council may from time to time make regulations with respect to any of the following matters or for any of the following purposes:

Regulations.

(i)   The administration of the affairs of the College;

(ii)   The conditions of appointment, services and termination of service of officers, teachers and employees;

(iii)   The establishment, conduct and control of a provident or superannuation fund;

(iv)   The form of conduct;

(v)   College Publications;

(vi)   Fees;

(vii) The conduct of elections to such officers or memberships as the Ordinance or Constitution prescribes shall be filled by election;

(viii) Generally, all matters which by this Constitution or the Post-Secondary College Ordinance Cap. 320 or any other relevant Ordinance it is empowered to regulate.

(2)   The Academic Board may from time to time make regulations with respect to any of the following matters and for any of the following purposes:

(i)   The admission, registration, residence, welfare

and discipline of students;

(ii)   The conditions for the award of College diplomas and College Certificates and other marks of distinctions;

(iii)   Courses of study and examinations;

(iv)   The award of scholarships, prizes and other educational endowments;

(v)   The use of College libraries, laboratories, workshops, museums and other institutions;

(vi)   Prescribing conditions under which persons may be exempted from the provisions of any regulations made by the Academic Board; and

(vii) Generally all matters which by this Constitution or the Post-Secondary College Ordinance, Cap. 320 or any other relevant Ordinance it is empowered to regulate.

(3)   Regulations made under sub-section (2) above shall not come into force until they have been approved by the College Council.

33.   Notwithstanding anything to the contrary hereinbefore contained *(a)* the following officers must be members of Hong Kong Baptist Churches affiliated with the Association:

(i)   The President;

(ii)   The Vice-President;

(iii)   The Dean of Studies;

(iv)   The Dean of Students;

(v)   The Chaplain;

(vi)   The Comptroller.

(b)   at least three quarters of the officers of the College and three quarters of the registered teachers employed by the College must be members of local Baptist or other Christian Churches.

34.   This Constitution may be amended by a resolution passed by a majority of the Board in two consecutive meetings, and also shall require the approval of The Execu-

Amendments of Constitution.

tive Board of the Association and the Director.

35.   This Constitution shall be subject to provisions of the Post-Secondary College Ordinance, Cap. 320 and all regulations thereunder.

Provisions of Post-Secondary College Ordinance, Cap. 320.

CONDITIONS OF SERVICE
HONG KONG BAPTIST COLLEGE

1. **College Principles.** The College is Christian in origin and purpose, and proposes to offer higher education in an atmosphere which is throughly Christian. Teachers and staff-members, by definite co-operation and example, are expected to uphold our Christian principles. It is further more hoped that each teacher and staff-member regularly attend a Church of his or her choice.

2. **Salary.** Teachers and staff-members shall receive the salary agreed upon by him (or her) at the time of appointment. The salary will be paid on or about the middle of each month.

3. **Activities, Responsibilities.** All teachers shall abide by the time, periods and subject assigned them and, when necessary, shall accept changes in the timetable. All staff-members shall fulfil the responsibilities assigned them and abide strictly by time and work schedules. Full-time teachers shall be prepared to teach fifteen semester hours per week. (Laboratory courses, where two class hours give one hour credit, and courses in which class hours may by more than credit hours, are assigned and paid for on the basis of credit hours.) Committee work and help in preparing and marking entrance examination and/or graduation examination papers, and help and co-operation in connection with extra-curricular activities, is expected of all full-time teachers and assistants.

4. **Full-time Faculty and Staff.**
    a. *All full-time staff and faculty,* including assistants, are expected to attend regular one weekly assembly of the College and the Faculty and Staff devotional meetings, unless definite arrangements are otherwise made.

b. *In addition to attendance at classes,* all full-time teachers shall arrange to stay in the College for a number of hours each week, so that they may be available for discussion and consultation with their students. Office hours shall be posted and provided the administration for reference.

c. *Full-time Devoted to College.* Full-time teachers and staff-members shall devote all their time to the College and shall not undertake any work outside the College without the previous approval in writing of the President and Vice-President. This includes private coaching.

d. *Absence from duty.* A teacher or staff-member shallrnot absent himself from duty except in accordance with leave granted by the administration of the school, or for reason of ill-health, in which case he shall inform the administrative authorities as soon as possible.

e. *Lengthy absences.* A teacher or staff-member shall, in case of unavoidable absence exceeding four consecutive working days, arrange for substitute in consultation with the administrative officials. The person concerned is responsible for the remuneration paid to the substitute and shall inform the administration in writing of the arrangement.

5. **Part-time Lecturers:** Pay for part-time lecturing shall be reckoned in terms of the number of actual periods in class per week and paid for monthly on a ten month's basis. Pay for service shall be according to the contract between the teacher and the school. If classes are not attended due to personal reasons the monthly salary shall be reduced accordingly. Absence for personal reasons should be reported to the school authorities, if possible. Make-up periods, so reported to and announced by the school, may be paid for at the regular rate. Marking of papers and turning in grades promptly is expected of all part-time teachers.

6. **Appointments, resignations and termination of salaries:** All appointments are on a purely probationary basis for the first two years. On the completion of two full consecutive years of service, a lecturer or staff-member who signs a contract for the following year in which tenure is stipulated, may consider that he is on regular appointment. Regularly appointed faculty and staff-members who are no longer on probationary appointment will be asked annually to sign contracts approximately three months prior to the opening of school in September. All regular appointments are subject to annual approval by the Board of Trustees. Salaries shall commence from the date of assumption of full duties, and, on resignation, shall cease from the last day of performance of full duties.

7. **Termination of appointment by Notice:** During the first two years of full-

time service, and for all part-time teachers and staff-members, the appointment may be terminated by one month's written notice to be given by either party to the other. After the completion of two years of full-time service and after one has accepted regular appointment on tenure for the following year, three months' written notice by either party is required.

8. **Changes in the Conditions of Service:** The administrative officials may take such additions or amendments to these Conditions of Service as may be, from time to time, considered necessary, subject to the approval of the Board of Governors.